COOKING & THE
CROWN

TOM PARKER BOWLES

COOKING & THE CROWN

Royal recipes from
Queen Victoria to King Charles III

PHOTOGRAPHY BY JOHN CAREY
ILLUSTRATIONS BY ALICE PATTULLO

ASTER*

Contents

In memory of
Queen Elizabeth II

✴

For King Charles III
and Queen Camilla

Introduction

British royal food. For so long, the gilded pinnacle of gastronomy, a heady, regal extravaganza of excess, where course after exquisite course emerged from cavernous kitchens – borne aloft by liveried footmen on plates of pure gold – to sate the whims of the richest, most powerful people on earth. For these banquets were no mere dinner, rather soufflé diplomacy at its most subtle, as kings, queens and emperors, presidents, princes and prime ministers quietly shaped history over *Mousses de Merlan à la Dieppoise* and *Cailles Rôties sur Canap*é.

And it was here, at these glittering, candlelit feasts in ancient castles and grand palaces alike, that the great chefs of the age – Carême, Francatelli and the rest – were given the freedom (and budget) to create some of the most ornate, extravagant and complex dishes ever seen. The original haute cuisine, and the standard to which all other chefs aspired, this was cooking as both art and inspiration, an Entente Cordiale of British ingredients and French technique.

These days, though, few of us have the time, skill or inclination to debone a snipe, stuff a boar's head or roast a whole haunch of ox. Nor spend three days preparing *Consommé au Faisan avec Quenelles*. Of course, back in the days of Queen Victoria and Edward VII, with a permanent kitchen staff of forty-five, anything was possible and everything expected. But as the years passed, brigades grew smaller, and lunches and dinners less, well, exhausting. Now, the King and Queen are positively abstemious. And although state banquets are still as important as ever, a direct link to the gilded gastronomic heights of the good old days, they never go on for more than three courses, plus coffee, fresh fruit and petits fours.

This book, first and foremost, will be a tome for everyday use. I've spent months combing through archives, letters, diaries, cookbooks and biographies to glean recipes that appeal to the modern cook. And don't require an entire kitchen brigade. Contrary to popular legend, it wasn't all lark's tongues and roast cygnet – although the latter was an occasional Christmas dish. No, the royal family, from Victoria onwards, have tastes like everyone else. Victoria was a devotee of cake, fruit and all things sweet. Edward VII loved roast beef and Irish stew, George V liked curry, and mashed potato with everything, while his son, George VI, preferred his omelettes plain and unencumbered.

Of course, there are more recipes from the reigns of Queen Victoria and her son, Edward VII, as both were hearty eaters, and ruled at a time when lavishly rich ten-course lunches and twelve-course dinners were par for the course. George V, in contrast to his father, had relatively simple tastes, although his wife, Queen Mary, was, in the words of royal chef Gabriel Tschumi, one of the 'last great connoisseurs of food in England'. Their son,

George VI, was also a man who liked things straight and unadorned. And Queen Elizabeth II, while deeply knowledgeable about menus, special dishes and state banquets (she never forgot a favourite dish eaten by any guest), had tastes that were many miles removed from extravagant.

As for King Charles III, I could write a whole different book on his knowledge of, and support for, British food and farming. In fact, there is no one better informed on everything from rare breeds and heritage fruit and vegetables to cheesemaking, butchery and brewing. He is a genuine British food hero.

But if food is a prism through which one can see history and economics, then the cooking of the royal family offers a fascinating glimpse into the lives and habits of British society's upper strata. From the grand, if admittedly dyspeptic, excess of the Victorian and Edwardian ages, when cream, butter, foie gras and truffles were used with giddy abandon, to wartime parsimony (no booze, and a mere two courses at breakfast!) and on into the modern world. Recipes are predominantly British and French (as French cooking was long seen as superior, at least in court circles), with occasional forays into India, Germany and Italy. Not just a snapshot of the cooking of kings and queens, but a peek behind the scenes, an insight into royal kitchens, banquets, picnics and barbeques. A taste of royal life.

Most of all, though, this is a book about pleasure, the joys of cooking and eating, of sitting down together and breaking bread. It's a celebration of the seasons, of great British ingredients, and a few French ones too. You may be surprised at the simplicity of many of the recipes. That's the point. Food is the great leveller. I want to strip away the pomp and circumstance, and get right to the meat of the matter – a collection of wonderful recipes that you really want to cook, from over two centuries of regal eating.

Eat, drink and be merry. Oh, and God Save the King and Queen!

Tom Parker Bowles

Coat of Arms

This is the Royal Coat of Arms of the United Kingdom, although a different version is used in Scotland. The lion (representing England) and unicorn (representing Scotland) are 'supporters'. They're 'rampant' (or 'rearing up') but the tongues are merely decorative. There are four quarters on the Shield: two are the three lions of England (gold on red), then a red lion for Scotland and a harp for Northern Ireland. The whole arms are surrounded by the Garter, inscribed with the motto of The Order of the Garter, *honi soit qui mal y pense*. Or 'Shamed be whoever thinks ill of it'.

Royal Family Tree

This is a hugely simplified Royal family tree, concentrating, as this book does, on the British sovereigns, along with their husbands or wives. Because it would take page upon page to list the descendants of Victoria and Albert's nine children. Let alone the rest. Indeed, at one point, it seemed that most of Europe's royal families were related to Victoria. But as mother-in-law to the German Emperor, and grandmother to Tsar Nicholas II, it's easy to see how she earned her nickname as 'The Grandmother of Europe'.

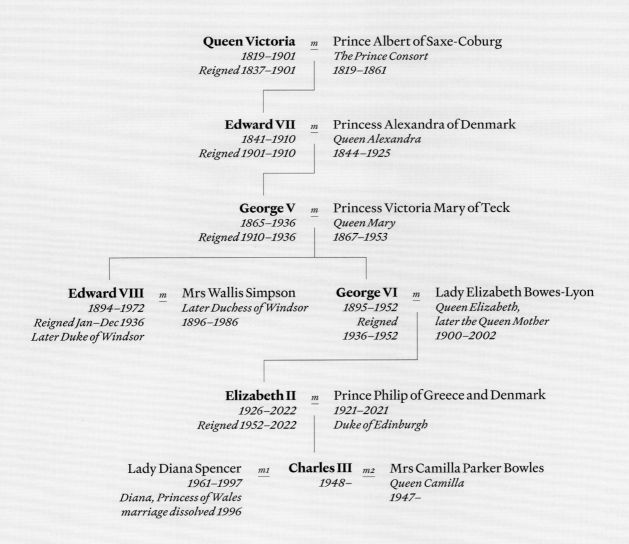

Queen Victoria *m* Prince Albert of Saxe-Coburg
1819–1901 *The Prince Consort*
Reigned 1837–1901 *1819–1861*

Edward VII *m* Princess Alexandra of Denmark
1841–1910 *Queen Alexandra*
Reigned 1901–1910 *1844–1925*

George V *m* Princess Victoria Mary of Teck
1865–1936 *Queen Mary*
Reigned 1910–1936 *1867–1953*

Edward VIII *m* Mrs Wallis Simpson
1894–1972 *Later Duchess of Windsor*
Reigned Jan–Dec 1936 *1896–1986*
Later Duke of Windsor

George VI *m* Lady Elizabeth Bowes-Lyon
1895–1952 *Queen Elizabeth,*
Reigned *later the Queen Mother*
1936–1952 *1900–2002*

Elizabeth II *m* Prince Philip of Greece and Denmark
1926–2022 *1921–2021*
Reigned 1952–2022 *Duke of Edinburgh*

Lady Diana Spencer *m1* **Charles III** *m2* Mrs Camilla Parker Bowles
1961–1997 *1948–* *Queen Camilla*
Diana, Princess of Wales *1947–*
marriage dissolved 1996

Breakfast

Breakfast

'To eat well in England,' the writer Somerset Maugham once joked, 'you should have breakfast three times a day.' He may have had a point. Because the aristocratic breakfasts of Victorian and Edwardian times were not so much dainty repasts as full-on gastronomic assaults, gut-busting epics that set one up for a good old-fashioned day's hunting, shooting and roistering. Or simply getting on with ruling one's realm.

Breakfast was served in silver chafing dishes, warmed with flickering spirit lamps. And this was the one meal where guests were expected to serve themselves. Well, with the obvious exception of sovereigns. Harold Nicolson, the upper-class polymath, described a typical upper-class spread of 'hams, tongues, galantines, cold grouse, ditto partridge, ditto ptarmigan ... the porridge would be disposed of negligently ... then would come the whiting, and omelette, and devilled kidneys and little fishy messes in shells. And then scones and marmalade. And then a little melon, and a nectarine, and just one or two of those delicious raspberries.' Breakfasts were, he noted wryly, 'in no sense a hurried proceeding'. OK, so life back then was rather less sedentary, and a lack of central heating meant extra calories helped keep one warm. Still, it would take a hearty appetite to do such a feast justice. An appetite shared, fortuitously, by Queen Victoria and her son, Edward VII.

'I remember my surprise on coming down to the kitchens on the first day of my duties,' writes Gabriel Tschumi in his memoir, *Royal Chef,* 'to find that breakfast was as big a meal as the main meal of the day in Switzerland.' He started as an apprentice in the Buckingham Palace kitchen in April 1898, before going on to cook under Edward VII and George V, eventually ending up as royal chef to Queen Mary. Seeing that lunch and dinner were usually ten courses long, he expected that 'breakfast would be a very light meal indeed'. How wrong he was. 'I found, instead, that the coal ranges were red-hot and the spits packed with chops, cutlets, steaks, bloaters [whole smoked herring], sausages, chicken and woodcock. The roast chefs were deftly removing them and piling them onto huge platters. In other parts of the kitchen cooks were trimming rashers of streaky bacon, a quarter of an inch thick for grilling, and preparing egg dishes.' The royal family would expect at least five dishes, as did the ladies- and gentlemen-in-waiting, who ate separately. 'Any servant could have the same number of courses for breakfast,' he noted. 'Quite a number managed it daily without any trouble.'

Queen Victoria enjoyed eating her breakfast *en plein air* in a tent on the lawn at Frogmore, in Windsor, and at Balmoral. Usually accompanied by the wheeze of bagpipes played by her personal piper – a tradition that goes onto this day. As was typical of contemporary accounts pertaining to the Queen, she was portrayed as having a suitably dainty appetite. 'The Queen's breakfasts are even plainer than her luncheons,' says the anonymous author, thought to be a high-ranking courtier, of *The Private Life of the Queen*. 'Fish is always on the table, but eggs on toast, or merely boiled, with dry toast and a small selection of fancy toast, are the usual articles put before the Queen at her first meal.' The author also notes that 'the eggs served at the Queen's breakfast table are exclusively those of white Dorkings', from her flock at Windsor.

In Scotland, in autumn of 1842, on her first visit to Scotland, 'Her Majesty took oatmeal porridge at breakfast, tried the "Finnan haddies," and pronounced the homely Scottish fare excellent.' Despite the popular myth, there's no evidence of breakfast curries, although after she was crowned Empress of India, two Indian retainers were always at her side.

Victoria's son, Edward VII, was a magnificent eater, one of history's great trenchermen. As Sidney Lee, one of his many biographers, pointed out, with admirable understatement, the King 'never toyed with his food.' Yet at breakfast, he was unusually restrained. 'The King was no breakfast eater,' wrote Sir Frederick 'Fritz' Ponsonby, his equerry and assistant private secretary, 'having only a cup of coffee and a bit of toast.' The exception was made on shooting and racing days. Then, he'd devour small fried soles, bacon, egg (either poached or *en cocotte*, a great favourite of his wife, Alexandra, who was as slim as her husband was broad), haddock *à l'anglaise,* devilled roast chicken and a couple of *becassines sur canapés*, or roast woodcock on toast.

Edward's son, George V, was a markedly different character from his epicurean father. A staunch naval man, he'd have been content to survive on military rations, and was dependably 'regular' in his habits. Five days a week, he ate eggs, crisp streaky bacon and fish, either trout, plaice or sole. On Saturdays, sausages too, 'basted and well-grilled'. The only time he strayed from this routine was when Yarmouth bloaters were in season. These replaced the bangers. His son, George VI, shared his father's restraint. And the variety of food was not much helped by Second World War rationing, which only ended in 1954, two years after his death.

Times change, along with appetites, although eggs still starred in the breakfasts of Queen Elizabeth II. Alongside orange juice, cereal and toast. When the royal family gathered at Balmoral or Windsor, there might be kedgeree, *oeufs en cocotte*, Benedict or Florentine. The King's breakfast is simply dried fruit and honey. Queen Camilla has yoghurt in summer and porridge in winter. A thoroughly modern, and healthy, start to the day. But I'm not sure Victoria would have approved.

Queen Camilla's Porridge

In winter, my mother, Queen Camilla, eats porridge every day – plain, aside from a little of her own honey. The hives sit at the back of a field at Raymill, the house in which my sister and I spent the latter part of our youth. During winter, all is quiet. But come the summer, we tend to give those hives a wide berth. My mother gives most of her honey to Fortnum & Mason, where it is sold in special jars, with all proceeds going to one of her charities. It's delicate and mild, as fine stirred into a good Darjeeling tea as it is mixed with porridge or yoghurt.

— Serves 1 —

50g rolled Scottish porridge oats

350ml full-fat milk

a pinch of salt

1 teaspoon honey

Put the porridge oats in a saucepan, add the milk and salt, and bring to the boil, then turn down the heat and simmer for about 5 minutes until thick and creamy.

Add the honey and serve.

Baked Eggs

Baked eggs, also known as *Oeufs en Cocotte,* have long been a staple of the royal table, from Queen Victoria to the present day. The Duke of Windsor was a particular fan. This was also a favourite dish from my childhood, usually devoured when we returned home from our holidays, when the fridge and larder were bare. My mother would use eggs from our chickens. Swap the ham or spinach for steamed asparagus, when in season.

— Serves 2 —

2 tablespoons of chopped ham or cooked spinach

4 eggs

2–3 tablespoons double cream

4 teaspoons butter

salt and freshly ground black pepper

hot toast, to serve

You will need
2 ovenproof ramekins

Preheat the oven to 180°C/350°F/gas mark 4.

Divide the ham or spinach between the two ramekins. Break the eggs into the ramekins (keep them whole), then add the cream and butter (half in each ramekin), and season with salt and pepper.

Put the ramekins in a small roasting pan and pour some just-boiled water into the base of the pan to come halfway up the sides of the ramekins. Bake for 7–10 minutes until the yolks are wobbling, and the whites are just set.

Serve with toast.

Devilled Kidneys

To our lily-livered modern tastes, kidneys on toast – made fiery (or 'devilled') with mustard, Tabasco and Worcestershire sauce – may seem a rather, well, punchy way to start the day. But you won't be surprised to hear that Edward VII devoured these with relish. And there's little doubt they provide splendid ballast for a long day's shooting, racing or reigning. I use lambs' kidneys, but veal are also divine.

— Serves 2 —

6 lambs' kidneys, about 350g total weight

3 tablespoons plain flour

1 teaspoon cayenne pepper

1 teaspoon mustard powder

2 teaspoons butter

6 tablespoons chicken stock

a lusty jig of Tabasco sauce

1 teaspoon Worcestershire sauce

salt and freshly ground black pepper

2 slices of white toast, to serve

Snip the white cores out of the kidneys using scissors and discard. Rinse the kidneys under cold running water, then drain and pat dry with kitchen paper.

Mix the flour, cayenne, mustard powder and some salt and pepper together on a plate. Dust the kidneys in the seasoned flour and shake to remove any excess.

Heat a frying pan over a medium-high heat, add the butter and fry the kidneys for 2 minutes on each side, or until cooked.

Add the stock, Tabasco and Worcestershire sauce, to taste.

Remove the kidneys from the pan and keep warm. Continue to simmer the sauce for a minute or two until reduced slightly.

Serve the kidneys on toast with the sauce poured over.

Kippers

Although the kipper has long been a regular dish on the royal table, it was fried fish (whiting or sole) that was eaten more frequently. But you can't beat a good kipper, and the Duke of Windsor was so devoted to these smoked herrings that he ordered Craster kippers every day from Fortnum & Mason – to be delivered by aeroplane to Château de Candé in France, where he lived in exile. There's nothing quite like the taste of home. Anyway, some are put off by the fiddly bones (properly filleted, there should be none), or the robustly fishy smell, which can be avoided by gently poaching in simmering water for 4 minutes. But I like them grilled, with a blob of butter gently melting on top. Manx kippers are particularly good, especially from L. Robson & Sons. For those who prefer a rather more gentle smoke, try Gloucestershire's Severn & Wye Smokery.

— Serves 2 —

2 kippers	2 sprigs of curly parsley
a dribble of olive oil	1 lemon, quartered
2 nuggets of butter	

Preheat the grill to high. Line the grill pan with foil, place the kippers on top with a dribble of olive oil, and grill for 4–5 minutes.

Anoint the fish with butter and, if you're feeling particularly baroque, a sprig of curly parsley. Allow to melt, then serve with a quarter of lemon to squeeze on top.

Rationing

1914. The start of the First World War, and the beginning of the end for Edwardian excess. As rationing began to bite, King George V and Queen Mary were determined to lead from the top. Lunch would be cut to a mere three courses, and meat served no more than three times a week. Breakfast, too, was ravaged. Where once there were silver chafing dishes filled with kippers, kidneys and kedgeree, there were now only two courses, decided by Queen Mary and ordered the night before. 'If anyone was tempted to help themselves to fish when they also had sausage and bacon,' remembered Gabriel Tschumi, 'one look from her was sufficient to make them change their minds.'

Sir Frederick Ponsonby tells the tale of one poor equerry, arriving late to breakfast and finding the table bare. He rang the bell for a boiled egg. 'If he had ordered a dozen turkeys, he could not have made a bigger stir.' The King accused him of being 'a slave to his inside, of unpatriotic behaviour, and even went so far as to hint that we should lose the war on account of his gluttony.'

Chefs in the royal kitchen tried their best to make things interesting. Fish and vegetables provided the backbone, the former fried or, in the case of smoked haddock, puréed and made into Toast Ivanhoe. Endless mutton 'cutlets' (made with minced mutton and cheap filling), eggs every way and vegetable pie did not go down well, either upstairs or down. Worse still, the King had decided that 'the use of alcohol was not consistent with emergency measures for winning a war', meaning there was to be no wine served at royal meals, or used in the kitchen either. The Queen was asked what people should drink with their food. 'Serve water boiled with a little sugar in the dining room,' came the curt reply. And that was that.

The King was not best pleased when his Prime Minister, Lloyd George, persuaded him to go teetotal and set a good example. Despite being a moderate drinker, 'I hate doing it,' he wrote in his diary, 'but hope it will do good.' No one really seemed to care. Which annoyed the King immensely. 'Balls to the whole thing,' was the view of his eldest son, who also told the story of his father retiring alone to his study after dinner every night, 'to attend to a small matter of business'. The 'business' being a small glass of port.

Rationing in the Second World War was taken every bit as seriously, although the meagre coupons were supplemented by game and vegetables (neither of which were rationed) from the royal estates. Fish, too, was off ration, but supply variable. The wedding breakfast, on 26 November 1947, of Princess Elizabeth and Lieutenant Philip Mountbatten was just four courses long, and over, they said, in twenty minutes. The wars may have been won. But the glory days of royal eating were forever lost.

Herrings Fried in Oatmeal

A classic breakfast dish and one much enjoyed, like most dishes, by Edward VII. Herrings are cheap, sustainable, filled with lots of lovely omega-3 fatty acids and taste divine. What's not to love?

— Serves 2 —

4 herrings, cleaned and boned, with head and tail removed

75g butter, melted

250g oatmeal (medium, if possible)

salt and freshly ground black pepper

To cook

100g butter

juice of 1 lemon

a dash of Tabasco sauce

Dip the herrings in the melted butter, season, then roll in the oatmeal to coat.

Heat the butter in a frying pan until it is foaming, then cook the herrings for about 2–3 minutes on each side. Remove the fish from the pan to serving plates.

Add the lemon juice and Tabasco to the butter in the pan, swirl it around a bit, then pour over the herrings to serve.

Haddock à l'Anglaise

Haddock, English-style. Much loved during the 'Golden Age' of the English breakfast, this was just one of many fish dishes to grace the royal table. And while *à l'anglaise* can mean a multitude of different things (battered, baked, poached, grilled, and so on), it usually refers to something simply served, perhaps with a basic butter sauce. I've used smoked haddock here, as it seems more suited to breakfast.

— Serves 2 —

300g undyed, smoked haddock, skinned (not that garish, neon-yellow stuff, if possible – go to your local fishmonger)

250ml full-fat milk

2 eggs

50g butter

juice of 1 lemon

a handful of parsley, chopped

salt and freshly ground black pepper

Poach the haddock gently in the milk over a medium heat for about 5 minutes, until the fish is tender and cooked through. Remove the fish from the pan and quickly pat dry on kitchen paper. Remove any bones, cover and keep warm.

Meanwhile, poach the eggs (and with poached eggs, the fresher the better). Bring a pan of heavily salted water to the boil. Break each egg into a ramekin. When the water is gently boiling, create a whirlpool by stirring the water with the handle of a wooden spoon. Slide one egg at a time into the whirlpool, turn down the heat to simmering and cook the eggs for 3–4 minutes, or until the egg whites are firm but the yolks are still runny. Remove the eggs with a slotted spoon and place carefully on a double layer of kitchen paper to drain.

Melt the butter in a small saucepan. When foaming, add the lemon juice and some freshly ground black pepper and stir to combine.

Place the haddock on two plates, top with the poached eggs and pour over the hot butter sauce. Sprinkle with chopped parsley and serve.

Kedgeree

Kedgeree is a breakfast classic, and one of the few Anglo-Indian dishes, along with mulligatawny, that endures. Descended from *khichri*, an Indian lentil and rice dish, it was made English by the addition of smoked haddock (or Finnan Haddies, which some say originally came from Findon in Aberdeenshire, while others claim Findhorn in Moray). During the Second World War, the Queen Mother substituted the haddock with salmon, which was off-ration, and which she caught herself. The key is a whisper, rather than a shout, of decent curry powder, while the fresh spices and herbs add their own gentle allure.

— Serves 4 —

400g smoked, undyed haddock

a big glug of olive oil

1 onion, finely chopped

2 green cardamom pods

1 teaspoon coriander seeds, dry roasted, then whizzed in a spice grinder or pounded in a pestle and mortar

1 teaspoon ground turmeric

1 bay leaf

1 tablespoon medium curry powder

300g basmati rice

500ml chicken or vegetable stock

5 tablespoons double cream (or crème fraîche, for a lighter taste with more acidic edge)

salt and freshly ground black pepper

To garnish

1 medium onion, sliced

20g butter

4 eggs, cooked for 5 minutes until soft-boiled, cooled, peeled and halved

a handful of coriander leaves, chopped

2 lemons, halved (optional)

Put the smoked haddock into a large pan, cover with water and bring to a simmer, then remove and break into fat chunks, discarding any skin and bones. Set aside.

Preheat the oven to 180°C/350°F/gas mark 4.

Heat the oil in a heavy-based casserole pan over a medium heat, add the onions and soften for about 10 minutes. Add the cardamom, ground coriander seeds, turmeric, bay leaf and curry powder, and cook for another 5 minutes.

Rinse the rice under running water until it runs clear. Add to the pan, mixing it with onions, and cook for about a minute, then add the stock, season well, cover the pan with the lid and transfer to the oven. Cook for 20 minutes, or until the rice is tender and all the stock has been absorbed.

While the rice is cooking, slowly fry the sliced onion for the garnish in the butter until golden brown, about 20 minutes. Drain on kitchen paper.

Once the rice is done, retrieve the cardamon pods and bay leaf and discard. Heat the cream or crème fraîche in a small pan, add the haddock and heat through for 2 minutes. Add it to the rice and check the seasoning.

Serve in one large serving bowl, or four individual ones, garnished with the fried sliced onions, egg halves and chopped coriander, with lemon halves for squeezing, if liked.

Lunch

Lunch

Lunch. For most of us, a snatched, sorry sandwich at the desk, or a rushed bowl of soup, slurped down between interminable Zoom calls. A blip, a pause, a brief stop for fuel. Which is a crying shame, because this is the most civilised of meals, one of life's true pleasures, a time to step back, sit down and settle into a long, languorous feast, an escape from the strictures of everyday life.

And the royal family, at least in Victorian and Edwardian times, took lunch very seriously indeed. 'At two o'clock came luncheon,' wrote Sarah Tooley in 1897, 'at which the Queen ate and drank heartily after her morning's work.' But while a decent lunch these days might stretch to three courses, one eaten with Victoria or Edward VII required the stamina of an ox. 'A good digestion was essential in those days,' noted Gabriel Tschumi, 'when each meal was equivalent to a present-day banquet. There was never any fear of Queen Victoria's guests leaving the table hungry.'

Lunch would always start with a soup, either thick pottage or a clear, consommé-style broth that seemed simple enough, but required a few days preparation. Followed by fish, meat and dishes both simple (plover's eggs, lobster salad) and more complex (*chaudfroid de poulets*); something roast (ortolans or fowls), vegetables and at least three puddings. Along with the ever-present sideboard packed with whole cold joints of meat.

Contemporary reports of the Queen's eating habits were, as ever, flattering. 'Her Majesty's tastes in food are most simple,' noted an anonymous courtier. Before going on to describe her sparrow-like appetite – for lunch, little more than a tiny slice of boiled chicken, or a sliver of beef from the sirloin. The nearest our source gets to anything approaching indiscretion is that 'Her Majesty confesses a great weakness for potatoes.' While the Queen would not partake of every course, she was, as food historian Annie Gray points out in *The Greedy Queen*, 'a woman who could eat'. So all those gushing contemporary accounts of her dainty appetite should be taken with a great shovel of *fleur de sel*.

There were no such illusions about her son, Edward VII (known as Bertie to his family), who had truly heroic appetite. And while he didn't actually drink very much – a glass or two of Chablis, or dry champagne, or claret, with the occasional whisky and soda between meals – he most certainly could eat. For elevenses, lobster salad and cold chicken, and his ever-present flask of turtle soup. A lunch in honour of the Shah of Iran, held on HM Yacht *Victoria and Albert*, on 20 August 1902, was typical in its glorious excess – crayfish bisque and sole mayonnaise; lamb cutlets, chicken in tarragon sauce, roast grouse, dressed crab and cold meat in aspic, alongside various vegetables and puddings. But even this was positively spartan when compared to his 'picnic' lunches for the Derby and Ascot, packed into hampers at Windsor and ferried down to the racecourse. A typical lunch, on

19 June 1908, started with cold consommé, followed by crab mousse, salmon, chicken salad, lamb cutlets, hot ham, cold quails, asparagus, Eton mess with cherries, gooseberry fool, *patisseries à la Parisienne* and fruit. Alongside a cold buffet with pigeon pie (an Ascot tradition), cold joints of meat, salad and rum baba. It's a wonder anyone actually managed to get up from their chair, let alone watch any racing.

But Bertie was nothing if not democratic in his tastes. While he adored the truffle-strewn voluptuousness of classic French cuisine, he went from haute to hearty (roast beef and Yorkshire pudding were served every Sunday, while Irish stew, Scotch broth and steak pies were a shooting-lunch staple) in the twitch of a whisker.

After Edward VII, things became a little, well, subdued. At York Cottage, on the Sandringham Estate, where George V and Queen Mary lived until Queen Alexandra died, one guest was astonished to turn up to lunch to find the door opened by the King, and then sitting down to a relatively parsimonious lunch of roast pheasant and chocolate mousse. George was a creature of regimented habit, supping two bowls of chicken consommé every day at 11am. On his private menus (as opposed to the more formal, French-accented ones), his tastes were simple, solid and very British. Curries (he'd acquired a taste for them while in India), along with bluff, plain English comfort food – cutlets, cottage pie, game pie and roast beef.

Queen Mary, though, preferred more elaborate, haute dishes such as *Côtelettes de Saumon à la Montpelier*. But even she rarely ate more than two courses. Their son, George VI, father of the late Queen Elizabeth, shared his father's unfussy tastes. When he came to lunch at Marlborough House with Queen Mary, the menu was 'fairly simple and plain,' according to Tschumi, usually consisting of an omelette, chicken or cutlets and ice cream as dessert.

The Queen Mother's lunches, at Royal Lodge at Windsor, or Birkhall in Scotland, were jolly affairs. My father remembers lobster, salmon and 'lots of things in rich, creamy sauces'. Her page, William Tallon, was famously liberal with the wine. If you politely declined, putting your hand over your glass, he'd simply distract you, then top up with aplomb. Even if it meant pouring through your fingers.

The late Queen's tastes were simple. She was not, according to Mark Flanagan – Royal Chef to the late Queen and King Charles – a big eater and, if by herself, would often eat only one course. Queen Camilla's lunches are light: chicken consommé, or smoked salmon, while the King, on the other hand, does not eat lunch at all.

The Queen Mother's Gin & Dubonnet

Despite the vast and magnificently stocked cellars at both Windsor Castle and Buckingham Palace, the monarchs, from Queen Victoria to King Charles III, were not (and are not) great drinkers. The occasional glass, rather than endless bottles. And while the Queen Mother is affectionately remembered for liking the odd tipple – you'd certainly never go thirsty at one of her splendid lunches – it was more about being a generous host. This was a cocktail much appreciated by the late Queen and Queen Mother alike, sipped before lunch. It has a stirring mixture of sweet, bitter and vaguely herbal flavours. And certainly puts a spring in one's step.

— Makes 1 —

2 parts Dubonnet

1 part gin

4 cubes of good ice

a slice of lemon

Pour the booze into a tumbler with the ice and mix well. Garnish with the lemon slice.

Potage Parmentier

This recipe is a version of *Purée de Pommes de Terre, dite Parmentier*, and taken from Auguste Escoffier's *Guide Culinaire*, one of the most influential cookbooks of all time. Published in 1903, it's the bible of French haute cuisine, and contains recipes inspired by the royal family, including *Cerises Jubilee* for Queen Victoria's jubilee, and *Selle d'Agneau de Lait Edouard VII*. Escoffier also cooked for Edward VII at The Savoy, among many other members of the royal family. Named after French physician and potato evangelist Augustin Parmentier, it's a classic leek and potato soup. It was also a favourite of Queen Victoria, and appears on the menu of Her Majesty's Dinner in honour of her Diamond Jubilee, on Tuesday 22 June 1897. Naturally, I've adapted the recipe slightly for the modern cook. The double cream adds its usual lustrous depth, while the croutons provide crunch. Vegetable stock can be used to make this vegetarian.

— Serves 2 —

white parts of 2 freshly washed leeks, finely sliced into rings

25g butter

3 medium floury potatoes, peeled and quartered

500ml fresh chicken stock

salt and freshly ground black pepper

To garnish

a glug of double cream

2 tablespoons croutons

fresh chervil, chopped (you could also use a big pinch of chopped chives)

In a saucepan over a low heat, gently cook the leeks in the butter for about 10–15 minutes until soft.

Add the potatoes and stock, season with salt and pepper, and bring to a simmer, cooking for about 10–15 minutes until the potatoes are soft to the touch.

Transfer to a blender and whizz until smooth.

Pour into bowls, add cream and garnish with croutons and chopped herbs.

Queen Camilla's Chicken Broth

This is Queen Camilla's lunchtime staple. It's light yet sustaining and endlessly adaptable. In winter, carrots, thinly sliced cabbage and potatoes provide the ballast, while in spring and summer, broad beans, peas, spinach and runner beans take their place. But feel free to throw in whatever you like, from chopped artichoke hearts, to asparagus, swede, watercress and green beans. Serve with a thick slice of toasted brown bread.

— Serves 4 —

1.5 litres good dark chicken stock

2 chicken thighs, roasted, cooled and shredded

juice of 1 lemon

a lusty dash of Tabasco (optional)

a big pinch of salt

a big screw of black pepper

a handful of grated Parmesan, to serve (optional)

Winter

1 medium potato, finely diced and parboiled

1 carrot, finely diced

1 celery stick, finely diced

½ Savoy cabbage, thinly shredded

Summer

a handful of broad beans

a handful of peas (fresh or frozen)

a fistful of spinach, finely chopped

a handful of runner beans, thinly sliced

Bring the stock to the boil and reduce by a third, then add the shredded chicken.

Add the potato, carrot and celery (if using), and simmer for 3 minutes or so until tender, adding the cabbage for the final minute. If using broad beans, peas, spinach and runner beans, they only need a minute.

Add the lemon juice, Tabasco, if using, and seasoning.

Pour into four bowls, sprinkle with Parmesan, if using, and serve.

Asparagus

WITH SAUCE MOUSSELINE

In 1907, King Edward and Queen Alexandra entertained an esteemed Indian guest for dinner at Buckingham Palace. Asparagus was on the menu, as it always was when in season, served with a *sauce mousseline*. As they started to eat, the King noticed the man tucking in with gusto, eating the main part of the stalk, and tossing the woody stem over his shoulder. Rather than cause offense, the King quicky did the same, meaning the whole table swiftly joined in. By the end, there were numerous tiny piles of asparagus stems on the carpet behind the chairs. 'There were a few grumbles from those who had to report the stains,' notes Tschumi, 'but there was nothing but admiration for the King's quick-wittedness.' Seasonality has long been at the heart of royal eating (and, in fact, all eating before the advent of fridges and freezers), and there's much to be said for eating asparagus at the peak of its season, which starts in May and ends on the last day of Royal Ascot, sometime around mid-June. Like peas, the sugars convert quickly into starch, within hours of being harvested, so you want it as fresh as possible. *Sauce mousseline* (named after the light and airy texture of muslin) is simply hollandaise with whipped cream folded in at the end.

— Serves 4 —

24 asparagus spears
salt and freshly ground black pepper

For the sauce mousseline
250g butter
4 egg yolks

½ teaspoon white wine vinegar
1 small ice cube
a pinch of salt
a big squeeze of lemon juice
150ml whipping cream, whipped to soft peaks

Boil or steam the asparagus in a large pan of well-salted boiling water. Cook for 4–6 minutes until tender but not soft. Drain on kitchen paper and set aside.

Heat the butter in a pan and skim off the white solids. Keep warm.

Take a glass or metal bowl, add the egg yolks, vinegar, a small ice cube and a pinch of salt, and whisk for a minute. Set the bowl over a pan of gently simmering water and whisk until thick, about 4–5 minutes. Remove from the heat and slowly whisk in the melted butter. When nice and glossy, add the lemon juice.

Carefully fold the whipped cream into the sauce until all is homogenous. Pour over the asparagus, top with black pepper and serve immediately.

Crab Mousse

This recipe comes from 'Debo', Deborah Mitford, the late Dowager Duchess of Devonshire, a remarkable woman in every way. Chicken expert, Elvis fanatic and saviour of Chatsworth House (the Derbyshire seat of the Devonshires), she was – at least to this particular child – at once terrifying, hugely glamorous, funny and very kind indeed. She was also a dear friend of the King, and versions of this mousse have also appeared on the royal table. Don't be put off by all the ingredients (or the gelatine) – once you have the ingredients, it's just a case of putting everything together.

— Serves 4–6 —

2 leaves of gelatine

125ml chicken or vegetable stock

300g white crab meat, picked to remove any shell

150g mayonnaise

a pinch of cayenne pepper

a good dash of Tabasco

100ml double cream

1 tablespoon chopped chives

salt and freshly ground black pepper

thinly sliced brown toast, to serve

Soak the gelatine in a bowl of cold water for 5 minutes until the leaves have softened.

Heat half of the stock in a small saucepan or in the microwave until hot but not boiling. Remove from the heat, drain the gelatine, add to the hot stock and stir to melt. Add the remaining cold stock, mix to combine and leave to cool slightly.

In a bowl, mix together the crab, mayonnaise, cayenne pepper and Tabasco, and season well with salt and pepper. Add the stock mixture and stir to combine.

Whip the cream to soft peaks and fold into the crab mixture along with the chopped chives. Spoon into a serving dish, cover and chill for 3 hours, or until set.

Serve with thinly sliced brown toast.

Potted Crab

Potting is an old English method of preservation, described as 'medieval clingfilm' by food historian Bee Wilson, in which crab or brown shrimp, ham or beef is sealed under a layer of clarified butter. I've borrowed this recipe for crab from Tom Pemberton, the chef proprietor of Hereford Road in Bayswater, London. Simply because it's the best I've ever tasted. Crabs are available all year round but are at their best between March and November.

— Serves 6 —

250g brown crab meat and 250g white crab meat, picked to remove any shell

175g unsalted butter

a good pinch of cayenne pepper (vibrant red if possible, not orange and dusty from an old container that has lost its potency)

a good pinch of ground mace

2 pinches of freshly grated nutmeg

juice of ½ lemon

salt and freshly ground black pepper

To serve

toast

cucumber pickles (optional)

You will need

6 ramekins

In a bowl, fold together the brown and white crab meat with a spatula.

Melt 75g of the butter, add to the crab with the spices, season with salt and pepper, and fold together. Here, two kitchen tropes are relevant: taste as you add and taste again. The amounts are only guides – they cannot account for personal preference, or the age or strength of the spices used. Also, add incrementally: you can always add but you can't take away.

Squeeze in the lemon juice through a sieve to remove any pips, mix to combine, then taste again and adjust the seasoning, adding lemon juice accordingly. Spoon the mixture into six ramekins, level the tops with the back of a spoon, cover and refrigerate for 30 minutes.

Melt the remaining butter in a small pan over a low heat. When the fat and solids start to separate, remove from the heat before the butter browns. Pour into a jug and leave to rest until the milky solids have sunk to the bottom, then carefully spoon off the yellow clarified butter from the top and pour over the potted crab to seal. Cover and chill for at least 1 hour until set.

Eat within three days and enjoy with toast and, if you like, cucumber pickles to cut the richness.

Crab with Sauce Remoulade

There are surprisingly few, if any, crab recipes in the books of Francatelli and Escoffier. Perhaps it was seen as the poor cousin of the more noble lobster (although I'm not sure why), and thus seen as unfit for royal bellies. But by the time Edward VII reached the throne, it scuttled onto centre stage, where it remains to this day. This dish was served to George V at Ascot on 16 June 1922. You can make your own mayonnaise, which is not hard. But because the flavours here take no prisoners, Hellmann's is just fine.

— Serves 2 —

white and brown meat from 1 whole brown crab, picked to remove any shell

thinly sliced white toast, to serve

1 lemon, quartered, for squeezing

For the sauce remoulade

350ml mayonnaise

1 tablespoon finely chopped capers (non-pareil, if you can find them)

1 tablespoon chopped gherkins

1 tablespoon finely chopped tarragon

1 tablespoon finely chopped parsley

3 tinned anchovy fillets, drained and finely chopped

2 tablespoons Dijon mustard

freshly ground black pepper

Mix all the sauce ingredients together.

Arrange the white crab meat along with the brown on two plates. Put a large blob of sauce on the side of each. Serve with thin white toast and a squeeze of lemon.

Lobster Salad

Another summer classic, found as often at Ascot lunches and Royal Opera House dinners, as it was at Castle of Mey lunches and picnics with the Queen Mother. Of course, lobster doesn't come cheap, so this is somewhat of a treat.

— Serves 2 —

1 medium lobster, cooked, hewn in half, tail meat removed and cut into 2.5cm medallions, knuckles cracked and meat removed, claws tapped with the back of a heavy knife so the flesh can be easily slipped from the shell

1 lemon, quartered, to serve

For the sauce

150ml mayonnaise

45g ketchup

a hearty shake of Tabasco

a good jolt of Worcestershire sauce

a generous pinch of cayenne pepper

a small dribble of brandy

For the salad

3 whole baby gem lettuces, washed, dried and sliced into strips

1 whole avocado, diced

½ cucumber, deseeded and diced

2 tomatoes, skinned, deseeded and diced

salt

For the dressing

3 tablespoons extra-virgin olive oil

2 tablespoons white wine vinegar

1 tablespoon fresh lemon juice

salt and freshly ground black pepper

Make the sauce by mixing all of the ingredients together in a large bowl. Add all the lobster meat, except the claws, to the sauce and mix well.

Mix the lettuce, avocado, cucumber and tomato in a bowl. Season with salt.

Mix the dressing ingredients in a jam jar and shake to combine, then mix with the salad. Divide the salad between two cocktail glasses.

Spoon the lobster mixture on top of each and top with a claw. Serve with a quarter of lemon, for squeezing, if liked.

Smoked Eel Mousse

This recipe comes from Gavin Rankin, the ever-elegant proprietor of Bellamy's in Mayfair, which was one of the late Queen's favourite restaurants. She had impeccable taste. Now try as I might, Gav is far too discreet to tell me what she ordered. 'She might have eaten the smoked eel mousse more than once, but that is something that I can neither confirm nor deny.' Actually, Gavin didn't come up with the actual recipe. He leaves all the cooking to his marvellous Executive Chef Stéphane Pacoud, while this particular patron gets on with the serious business of *mange*-ing *ici*. If you don't have seafood consommé (few do), feel free to use a shellfish or fish stock. It won't taste quite as rich, but saves an awful lot of bother.

— Makes 6 —

220g Devon smoked eel fillets

100g mayonnaise

250g whipped cream

2 gelatine leaves

100ml hot seafood consommé (or fish/lobster/prawn stock)

toast, to serve

You will need

6 × 7cm ramekins

Mince the smoked eel with the mayonnaise in a food processor until very fine. Transfer to a bowl and add the whipped cream to the mix.

Melt one of the gelatine leaves in a small pan over a low heat, then add the melted gelatine to the bowl of smoked eel mixture. Mix together until well combined.

Fill the ramekins three-quarters full with the mousse and leave to settle in the fridge for 1 hour.

Add the second gelatine leaf to the consommé (or stock) and mix to combine, then allow to cool to room temperature. Top up each ramekin to a depth of 5mm, about 3 teaspoonfuls per ramekin, of consommé. Leave in the fridge to set for another hour. Serve with thin, white toast.

Truites Froides au Rubis

This sea trout dish was served at Edward VII's Epsom lunch party in 1909. A mustard-keen racing man, it was the year that his horse, Minoru, won the Derby, making him the first reigning British monarch to achieve this legendary accolade. There is no bigger race to win in the world, so that day must have been very jolly indeed. Lunches both at Ascot and Epsom were typically lavish affairs. I tend to avoid salmon these days, as the farming industry is both environmentally ruinous and produces a pretty second-rate fish, too. Sea trout is far superior in every way to the sad, flabby and fatty farmed beasts. To keep stocks sustainable, sea trout is not available in the UK during the closed season (1 November –2 April), so if you're cooking this during the colder months, use farmed trout instead.

— Serves 8 —

400ml dry white wine

1 celery stick, sliced

1 small leek, quartered

1 onion, thickly sliced

1 lemon, quartered

2 bay leaves

½ bunch parsley (stalks and all)

a large pinch of black peppercorns

1.5 litres water

1 whole sea trout, about 2kg, cleaned, with head and tail left on

2 egg whites plus the egg shells, roughly crushed

200ml claret or other full-bodied red wine

8 leaves of platinum-grade gelatine

To garnish

6 eggs, at room temperature

4 tablespoons mayonnaise

3 tomatoes, skinned and diced

¼ cucumber, deseeded and diced

dill sprigs

salt and freshly ground black pepper

In a fish kettle, combine the wine, celery, leek, onion, lemon quarters, bay leaves, parsley and peppercorns. (See note overleaf if you don't have a fish kettle.) Add the measured water, bring to the boil, then reduce the heat and simmer for 5 minutes. Remove from the heat and leave for 30 minutes to allow the aromatics to infuse the court bouillon.

Add the trout to the pan (add a little more water if needed to at least half submerge the fish), bring slowly to the boil, cover and simmer for 30 minutes until the fish is cooked through. Remove from the heat and leave the fish to cool in the pan.

When cold, carefully lift the fish from the pan and remove the skin and fins, but leave the heat and tail intact. Cover and chill again for at least 2 hours.

continued overleaf

While the fish is chilling, strain the cold court bouillon into a clean pan.

In a small bowl, whisk the egg whites until foamy, add to the saucepan with the crushed egg shells and bring the court bouillon slowly to the boil over a medium heat without stirring. Simmer for 1 minute, then remove from the heat and leave to settle for 5 minutes. By now, the egg whites will have cooked and risen to the top of the court bouillon, forming a crust or raft trapping all the impurities and oil.

Using a large spoon, carefully make a hole in the middle of the crust and slowly ladle the resulting clear stock into a muslin-lined sieve over a clean bowl. Pour into a jug – you will need 900ml. Add the red wine and mix to combine. Cover and leave to cool, then chill until completely cold.

Soak the gelatine leaves in a bowl of cold water for 5 minutes until soft and floppy. Heat 150ml of the court bouillon until just boiling either in the microwave or in a small pan. Drain the gelatine, squeeze out any excess water and add to the hot liquid. Whisk until combined and thoroughly melted.

Add the gelatine mixture back to the jug of cold court bouillon and whisk to combine. Chill until the mixture is thickening and just starting to set.

Pat the trout dry with kitchen paper, place on a large tray and slowly spoon one third of the jelly mixture over the body of the fish, leaving the head and tail uncovered. Return to the fridge for 30 minutes to set.

Repeat this a further two times, chilling in between layers until the fish is enrobed in a layer of jelly. If the pouring jelly mixture sets a little too firmly to spoon, simply warm to the correct consistency, being careful that it is not hot, otherwise it will melt the first layers of jelly already on the fish. Leave to set for at least 1 hour and then transfer the fish to a serving platter.

Meanwhile, prepare the garnishes. Cook the eggs in boiling water for 10 minutes to hard boil. Cool under cold running water, then peel and halve. Press the yolks through a fine-mesh sieve, mix with the mayonnaise and season well. Pipe or spoon the yolk mixture back into the egg white halves. Garnish the trout with the stuffed eggs, diced tomatoes, cucumbers and dill sprigs.

Note: If you don't have a fish kettle, ask your fishmonger, as some have fish kettles to hire. Failing that, double line a very large roasting tin with heavy-duty foil, allowing extra foil to drape over the sides. Add the fish poaching ingredients and simmer on the hob as per the recipe, and leave to cool and infuse. Reheat the court bouillon on the hob, add the trout, cover tightly with foil and cook in an oven preheated to 150°C/300°F/gas mark 2 for about 30 minutes until the trout is cooked. Leave to cool in the tin.

Salade Aida

This is a classic Escoffier salad, also made by Francatelli for Queen Victoria. A rare moment of crisp, green respite in the midst of all that butter and cream.

— Serves 4 —

4 red endives (or chicory), washed and separated into leaves

4 artichoke bottoms, sliced about 5mm thick (or 12 bottled artichoke hearts, sliced)

2 green peppers, deseeded and sliced about 5mm thick

4 eggs, boiled for 8 minutes, then shelled. Then the yolk removed and set aside.

For the dressing

6 tablespoons good extra-virgin olive oil

2 tablespoons red wine vinegar

1 teaspoon Dijon mustard

salt and freshly ground black pepper

Arrange the vegetables in a big bowl. Remove the egg yolks from the boiled eggs, slice the egg whites and add to the bowl, then crumble the egg yolks and scatter on top. Put the dressing ingredients into a jam jar, put the top on and shake well until emulsified. Mix the dressing with the salad and serve.

Oeufs Suzette

This was a dish served to George V, recovering from septicaemia and an abcess on his lung, when convalescing in the brisk Bognor sea air. 'Bugger Bognor' were said to be his last words, uttered in response to his doctor, who promised that he would soon be well enough to recuperate in the Sussex seaside town. If only it were true. The reality is rather more prosaic. The people of Bognor had asked if they could rename the town Bognor Regis, in honour of his stay. 'Bugger Bognor,' he growled to his private secretary, Arthur Stamfordham. Nevertheless, their wish was granted. Convalescent dishes were plain and easily digestible, involving all manner of beef jellies, chicken custards and a thousand ways with eggs. Despite the simplicity of these dishes, their preparation was usually anything but. The original recipe contains béchamel sauce, but with all the butter and cream involved it's an embellishment too far.

— Serves 4 —

4 medium baking potatoes, washed	8 thin slices of ham
100g butter	4 eggs, poached
100ml milk	a handful of Gruyère or Comté cheese
100ml double cream	
a big pinch of salt	crisp green salad, to serve

Preheat the oven to 220°C/425°F/gas mark 7.

Bake the potatoes for 1 hour until the skins are deep brown and crisp. When cool enough to handle, slice off the tops and scoop the soft flesh out into a bowl. Add the butter, milk, cream and salt, and mix together.

Heat the grill to high.

Line the inside of each potato shell with two slices of ham, then spoon the potato mixture back into the shells, leaving a good 5cm gap at the top of each. Add the poached eggs, top with the cheese, then brown under the fierce grill and top with black pepper.

Serve with a crisp green salad.

Fish Goujons

WITH TARTARE SAUCE

Another timeless and eternal royal favourite, this is fried fish with a thick French accent. Dover sole would have been traditionally used, but it does seem an awful waste. I tend to use haddock or plaice but even pollack, that rather dreary but eminently sustainable fish, will do.

— Serves 4 —

For the goujons

150g white bread, a couple of days old, no crusts (or panko breadcrumbs)

100g plain flour

2 eggs, beaten

500g white fish (sole, cod, haddock, plaice or pollack, filleted and skinned), cut into strips somewhere between the size of your small and ring fingers

sea salt and freshly ground black pepper

3 tablespoons olive oil, for frying

1 lemon, cut into wedges, to serve

For the tartare sauce

125g mayonnaise

a pinch of mustard powder

1½ tablespoons capers, finely chopped

2 tablespoons cornichons, finely chopped

1 small shallot, finely chopped

1 tablespoon chopped flat-leaf parsley

Make the tartare sauce by mixing all of the ingredients in a bowl. Set aside.

Tear the bread into small pieces and blitz in a food processor to make crumbs, then put them on a plate. Mix the flour with a little salt and pepper, and lay out on another plate. Put the eggs in a shallow dish. Using one hand (this stops both hands getting clagged up), dip the fish strips into the flour, then the egg, then the breadcrumbs, shaking off any excess at each stage.

Heat the olive oil in a large frying pan over a medium-high heat. When hot, fry the fish in batches until crisp and golden, then drain on kitchen paper. Keep hot while cooking the rest.

Serve with the lemon wedges and a great big dollop of tartare sauce.

Salmon Fishcakes

This was a typical lunch dish for Queen Elizabeth II, always made with salmon and mashed potato, then dipped in breadcrumbs and fried in butter. Once done, a 'neat circle' would be sliced from the top and a small indentation made, to allow a poached egg to sit snugly on top. Hollandaise sauce was then poured over. For a breakfast version, substitute 150g of the salmon with 150g smoked haddock.

— Makes 4 —

500g floury potatoes, boiled until soft, cooled and skins removed

3 tablespoons salted butter

100ml milk

300g boneless, skinless salmon fillets

a splash of white wine

2 teaspoons tomato ketchup

a handful of chopped flat-leaf parsley

zest of ½ unwaxed lemon

3 tablespoons plain flour, seasoned

2 eggs, beaten

100g dried breadcrumbs

4 eggs, poached

300ml hollandaise sauce (omit the whipping cream from the Sauce Mousseline recipe on page 39)

peas, to serve

salt and freshly ground black pepper

Make mashed potato by passing the cooked potatoes through a potato ricer into a bowl, then beat in 1 tablespoon of the butter and the milk. Season and set aside.

Preheat the oven to 220°C/425°F/gas mark 7.

Place the salmon on a large piece of kitchen foil, add the white wine and season with salt and pepper, then wrap into a loose parcel and place on a baking tray. Bake for 10 minutes, then remove, open the parcel and leave to cool.

Flake the salmon into the mashed potato and add the ketchup, parsley and lemon zest. Mix well, then form the mixture into four round cakes.

Put the flour, eggs and breadcrumbs into three separate bowls. Dip each cake first in flour, then into the eggs and finally the breadcrumbs.

Get the remaining 2 tablespoons of butter foaming in a heavy frying pan, then gently fry the cakes for 5 minutes on each side until golden. Remove to a plate lined with kitchen paper. Slice the top of each fishcake off and make an indention in the exposed surface.

To plate up, add a poached egg to the top of each fishcake, drown in hollandaise sauce and add freshly ground black pepper before serving with the peas.

Bounty from the Royal Estates

'In spite of the vast resources at her command for the raising of food under artificial conditions,' wrote an anonymous courtier, of Queen Victoria, 'she never permits her own table or that of Her Household to be served with anything that is out of season.' Royal menus, whether private or public, have always been in thrall to the seasons. Through necessity, in Victorian times. And then, as ice boxes transformed into freezers, and fresh fruit began to fly in from across the world, for the pure delight of eating food at its very peak – asparagus in May, strawberries in June, grouse in August or pheasant in October. That annual wait made everything taste that much the sweeter. It still does.

Game has long been central to the royal diet, with grouse and venison from Balmoral, pheasant and partridge from Sandringham, and rabbit, snipe, hare and blackcock from various royal lands across the country. Wild salmon was caught on the Dee, and trout in freezing mountain lochs. The estates have always provided all the fruit and vegetables, too – Windsor in particular. The glass houses at Frogmore in Victoria's day were a magnificent sight. She had eight 'pineries' – hothouses in which pineapples, the very apotheosis of exotic and extravagant eating (it took many thousands of pounds to produce just one fruit) were grown throughout the year. There were 250 different varieties of pear and the same of apples, 2,220 yards of outdoor asparagus beds, and an astonishing five miles of peas. Some 130 gardeners worked full time to keep kitchens supplied, and mighty appetites sated.

These days, things are a little more modest, although the royal kitchens still very much depend on the seasonal bounty of their farms and estates. The royal farm at Windsor, which supplies the palace kitchens as well as the farm shop, has a Sussex beef herd, a Jersey dairy herd, lambs, chickens and pigs. The late Queen even had her own double-cream cheese, made exclusively for her. King Charles has long been known for his passionate support of British food and farming. In fact, there has never been a sovereign with such a close, and fundamental, connection to the land. He was preaching for the seasonal, local and sustainable many years before they became the norm. And is not only fluent in the rural tongue, but a successful farmer himself. The link between land and sovereign is as strong as ever.

Poached Trout & Langoustine Salad

This salad was part of lunch at Buckingham Palace after the Coronation of Charles III, a particularly merry feast. We were mighty relieved (if not at all surprised) that this magnificent ceremony had gone so well. ChalkStream farmed trout is one of my favourite suppliers, as the fish are raised in waters with fast-flowing, clear water, meaning they don't have the usual muddy taste.

— Serves 10 —

1 large ChalkStream trout fillet (about 650g)

20–30 fresh langoustines (live is best, if you can find them)

10 quail's eggs

120g mixed leaf salad (depending on the season, I like to include a variety of strong-flavoured leaves: rocket, mizuna and watercress with added herbs, such as chervil and dill)

120g green beans, cooked

150g mi-cuit or sunblush tomatoes

1 lemon, for zesting

For the citrus vinaigrette

1 tablespoon lemon juice

1 tablespoon orange juice

1 teaspoon white wine vinegar

1 teaspoon Dijon mustard

4 tablespoons extra virgin olive oil

salt and freshly ground black pepper

For the court bouillon

400ml dry white wine

1 celery stick, sliced

1 small leek, quartered

1 onion, thickly sliced

1 lemon, quartered

2 bay leaves

½ bunch parsley (stalks and all)

a large pinch of black peppercorns

1.5 litres water

In a fish kettle or big pot, combine all the court bouillon ingredients, bring to the boil, then reduce the heat and simmer for 5 minutes. Remove from the heat and leave for 30 minutes to allow the aromatics to infuse.

Gently poach the trout in the court bouillon for about 10 minutes until the flesh is opaque. Carefully remove and allow to cool until you can gently handle it, mindful that the trout will be fragile.

Add the langoustines to the court bouillon in batches and boil for about 1½–2 minutes dependent on size. They are ready when the flesh on the undersides is white rather than translucent. Remove from the pan and stop the cooking by refreshing in iced water, but do not leave in cold water. Peel and set aside.

continued overleaf

Cook the quail's eggs in the court bouillon for 2½–3 minutes. Remove and set aside.

To make the citrus vinaigrette, lightly whisk all the ingredients together in a small bowl or shake together in a jam jar.

Gently toss the mixed salad leaves and herbs in three-quarters of the citrus dressing and arrange on a platter. Gently flake the trout into quite large, succulent pieces and arrange on and around the salad leaves. Season the langoustine tails with most of the remaining citrus dressing, ensuring they are well coated, and scatter over the salad. Add the cooked green beans and tomatoes. Peel the quail's eggs and slice in half, then dot around the salad. Use a microplane to finely grate a little lemon zest over the top of the salad to finish. Serve with extra dressing on the side.

✳

Grilled Sardines

Ah, the sweet scent of sardines grilling over coals, their salt-flecked skins blistering to reveal that rich flesh within. I'm not alone in my adoration. In 1925, the *Victoria and Albert* (the royal yacht with a crew of 300 and household staff of 30) sailed through the Mediterranean, starting at Genoa and on to Naples, Syracuse, Etna and Palermo, before sailing back to where they started. 'Every day we had sardines for luncheon,' recalls Tschumi. King George V grew very fond of these Mediterranean sardines and they were regularly served at Buckingham Palace.

— Serves 4 —

16 sardines, gutted and descaled	salt
olive oil	1 lemon, quartered, to serve

Either heat a barbecue to the point where the coals have a thin layer of white ash on top, or whack up the grill to maximum level.

Anoint the fish with olive oil and season well with salt. Cook over the barbecue or under the grill for 2–4 minutes per side, depending on size.

Serve with a squeeze of lemon.

Halibut en Papillote

This was another dish served after the Coronation of Charles III. It was the most momentous of days, but that lunch was surprisingly laid back (well, as laid back as lunch can be in Buckingham Palace), and very happy too.

— Serves 4 —

30g cold unsalted butter, plus extra for greasing

½ lemon, zested then sliced

50g shallots, sliced

1 bay leaf

2 large sprigs of fresh tarragon

½ piece of star anise

4 × 100–120g skinless, boneless halibut fillets (farmed)

200ml white wine

200ml fish stock

125ml double cream

finely chopped tomato and snipped chives, to garnish

salt and freshly ground black pepper

To serve

buttered new potatoes and seasonal vegetables (such as wilted spinach, broad beans, baby carrots, samphire or asparagus)

Preheat the oven to 180°C/350°F/gas mark 4.

Take a large sheet of kitchen foil, fold it in half to strengthen it and place on a baking tray. Generously butter the foil, then scatter with half of the lemon slices and shallots, adding the bay leaf, one tarragon sprig and the star anise. Top with the halibut portions, season with salt and pepper, then cover the fish with the remaining lemon slices, shallots and tarragon. Ensuring the edges of the foil form a slight bowl, add the white wine and fish stock, then cover the whole with another sheet of foil and roll up the edges to create a sealed packet, being careful not to make any tears or holes in the foil.

Cook in the oven for about 8–10 minutes, during which time the fish will have steamed and the foil puffed up to create a pillow. Remove from the oven and allow to rest for 3–4 minutes. Be careful of the steam when opening.

Carefully remove the fish from the packet, strain the remaining cooking juices into a saucepan and bring to a gentle boil. Add the cream and reduce to a thick sauce that just coats the back of a spoon. If necessary, thicken with a few knobs of the cold unsalted butter. Adjust the seasoning before serving.

Garnish the fish and sauce with the tomatoes and chives, and serve with buttered new potatoes and a selection of seasonal vegetables.

Saumon Chambord

The edible equivalent of Ozymandias' mighty boast, 'Look on my works, ye Mighty, and despair!' Invented by Francatelli, it was one of those extravagant showstoppers that not only proclaimed the genius and technical ability of the chef, but also used a glut of extravagant ingredients. Just, I suppose, because he could. A whole salmon was poached in champagne, before being skinned, speared by four crayfish, then girded with Dover sole fillets studded with truffles. At its base, whole black truffles, whiting quenelles stained pink by lobster coral, more crayfish and mackerel roe, all covered in *Espagnole* sauce and lashings of anchovy butter. Subtle, it ain't. It would have originally been made with wild salmon, one of the most magnificent of fish; lean, muscular and packed with flavour. The farmed version, though, is a sorry shadow of its noble cousin, not just flabby and pretty second rate, but environmentally ruinous too. I try to avoid it at all costs, but in writing a royal cookbook it's nigh on impossible to ignore. Either use sea trout, or go for the best-quality farmed fish you can find. I've slightly simplified the recipe (just for a change).

— Serves 4 —

4 × 150–175g thick salmon fillet portions, scaled and pin bones removed

300g small chestnut mushrooms, trimmed

4 shallots

2 sprigs of fresh thyme

2 bay leaves

400ml Burgundy

250ml fish stock

55g butter, diced

1 tablespoon plain flour

4 herring roes (optional, but recommended)

1 fresh black truffle, thinly sliced (very much optional)

salt and freshly ground black pepper

Preheat the oven to 180°C/350°F/gas mark 4. Place the salmon portions in a medium roasting tray lined with foil or baking paper. Roughly chop half of the chestnut mushrooms and all of the shallots and tip into the tray around the fish. Add the thyme sprigs and bay leaves, and season with salt and pepper. Pour in the wine and fish stock to almost cover the salmon. Cover and bake for about 25 minutes until the fish is just cooked. Carefully lift the salmon from the tray, remove the skin, then cover and keep warm.

Strain the cooking liquor into a saucepan, bring to the boil over a medium heat and reduce by half.

In a small bowl, cream together 2 teaspoons of the butter with 2 teaspoons of the flour to make a smooth paste or roux. Add the roux to the simmering sauce a little at a time, whisking

continuously until the sauce is smooth and has thickened slightly. You may not need to add the roux – the sauce should be just thick enough to lightly coat the back of a spoon.

Whisk another 20g of the butter into the sauce over a low heat until the sauce is smooth and glossy.

Melt the remaining 25g of butter in a frying pan, add the remaining whole mushrooms and cook over a medium-high heat until browned and tender. Remove from the pan and keep warm.

Season the remaining teaspoon of flour and dust the herring roes, if using, in it. Add to the hot frying pan and cook for about 30 seconds on each side until golden and cooked through.

Place the salmon on plates and divide the mushrooms and herring roes among them. Spoon over some sauce, keeping the remainder to put in a gravy boat, and finish with sliced truffles. Serve with the extra sauce alongside.

Fried Sole

WITH SHRIMP SAUCE

Dover sole, along with turbot and salmon, has been a mainstay of royal menus from Victoria onwards. Escoffier had hundreds of ways with Dover sole, but this recipe, adapted from one by Francatelli, advises using smaller specimens, as the big buggers are 'less likely to appear crisp, so essential a requisite in all fried fish'. The original recipe involves a shrimp sauce made with industrial amounts of butter and flour. I prefer things a little lighter, so have removed the flour and cut down on the dairy. Lemon, slip or megrim sole would be perfect. You need to ask the fishmonger to gut and skin them, and trim the fins too.

— Serves 2 —

100g plain flour, seasoned with a big pinch of salt and few twists of black pepper

2 eggs, beaten

100g fine breadcrumbs (panko are great)

4 tablespoons olive oil

100g unsalted butter

2 medium sole (lemon, megrim or slip)

For the shrimp sauce

100g unsalted butter

70g (or one packet) brown shrimp

juice of ½ lemon

a big pinch of cayenne pepper

a big jig of anchovy essence

a small pinch of salt

Place the seasoned flour, egg and breadcrumbs in three separate bowls.

Heat the oil and butter together in a large frying pan over a medium heat until the butter starts to foam.

Dip the soles in the flour, then into the egg, then the breadcrumbs. Place in the pan and fry for 4–6 minutes on each side, depending on size, until the skin is crisp and golden.

In another saucepan, melt the butter for the sauce over a medium heat until foaming, then add the shrimp, lemon juice, cayenne pepper, anchovy essence and salt. Cook gently for a few minutes, then pour over the cooked sole to serve.

Poulet Danoise

Queen Mary certainly knew her onions. Yet she also disliked 'extravagance of any kind and it displeased her if food at Marlborough House was ever wasted.' Not unlike her granddaughter and great grandson. This dish was her favourite. Tschumi suggests making your own 'nouilles' or noodles, but fresh tagliatelle will do fine, or even decent-quality packet stuff.

— Serves 4 —

1 large chicken, about 1.75kg

1 large onion, sliced

2 carrots, roughly chopped

1 bay leaf

300ml chicken stock (made with a decent stock cube is fine)

300ml double cream

juice of ½ lemon

1 packet of fresh tagliatelle (or other decent-quality dried pasta)

a little butter

salt and freshly ground black pepper

For the flavoured butter

200g butter, softened

2 tablespoons chopped parsley

juice of 1 lemon

Preheat the oven to 180°C/350°F/gas mark 4.

Flavour the butter by mixing it with the parsley and lemon juice, then put half inside the cavity of the chicken and smear the other half all over the outside of the bird. Season well with salt and pepper.

Put the chicken in a large, heavy casserole pot, along with the onion, carrots and bay leaf. Roast for about 1 hour 45 minutes, or until the juices run clear when you pierce the thickest part with the tip of a knife. Make sure it doesn't brown too much, so cover with foil if it is browning too quickly.

Take the chicken out and set aside to rest. Strain the pot juices through a sieve, skim off most of the fat, then simmer with the stock and cream to reduce. Season with lemon juice, salt and pepper.

Cook the pasta according to the packet instructions, then drain and toss with a little butter. Place on a serving platter.

Carve the chicken and lay on top of the noodles, then cover with the sauce and serve very hot.

Chicken Salad

This is a take on the classic chicken salad, eaten from Queen Victoria's day onwards. The good thing about a chicken salad is its adaptability, to both whim and season. Add what you want, remove what you don't. The usual royal recipe includes a great slick of mayonnaise, but I prefer the sharper, more subtle allure of a good vinaigrette.

— Serves 4 —

1 whole chicken (about 1kg), roasted (with lemon in cavity and heavily seasoned) for 1 hour, then rested for 20 minutes

a big lump of butter, for frying

4 garlic cloves, finely chopped

4 thick slices of sourdough, chopped into 2cm cubes

4 cos lettuces, washed and leaves separated

6 tomatoes, sliced

1 jar of artichoke hearts, drained

12 anchovy fillets

4 soft-boiled eggs with jammy yolks, halved

For the dressing

100ml white wine vinegar

1 tablespoon Dijon mustard

1 tablespoon Colman's mustard powder

300ml extra-virgin olive oil

salt and freshly ground black pepper

Roast your chicken first and leave it to rest.

To make the dressing, put the vinegar, Dijon, mustard powder, and a pinch each of salt and pepper into a bowl and whisk. Slowly add the olive oil and whisk until emulsified. Set aside.

Heat the butter in a small pan until foaming, then add the garlic and cook gently until soft. Add the cubed bread and fry until crisp. Remove the croutons with a slotted spoon to drain on kitchen paper.

Rip the chicken into good-sized chunks, making sure you get every last bit of meat off the bones. Reserve the carcass for stock. Place in a large serving bowl, then add the lettuce leaves, tomatoes, artichokes, anchovies, croutons and halved eggs. Mix well, then lavish with the dressing, ensuring every last bit is coated. Serve with extra dressing on the side.

Trio of Curries

The Royal Family have long been fans of a curry. But it's important to point out that these are very much anglicised recipes, more similar to the British curry house staples – which bear scant relation to the real thing – than the regional dishes of India, Pakistan and Bangladesh. That said, Victoria's Indian servants roasted and ground their own spices, as well as killing their own animals in accordance with religious law. So while the monarch's tastes were very westernised, Victoria's Indian attendants could cook and eat the real food of their homeland.

Elizabeth II's Curry

The late Queen was a curry lover, but her tastes, according to her Royal Chef Mark Flanagan, were assuredly mild. 'With the curry recipe for the late Queen Elizabeth,' Mark Flanagan tells me, 'we adapted a rather standard "British-style" curry recipe using a generic curry powder. Her Majesty preferred not to take chilli, or anything particularly spicy. Coconut was also a flavour that was not enjoyed. So we used to finish the curry using a more fragrant garam masala to elevate the base, using spices such as cinnamon, saffron and cardamom, then adding in natural yogurt and some freshly chopped flat-leaf parsley instead of coriander. As important as the curry,' he continues, 'were the condiments and accompaniments – these always included some diced cucumber, chopped tomato, mango chutney, well-cooked chopped shallots, some poppadoms and additional natural yogurt (just in case).' You can buy garam masala, but it always tastes so much better when you make it yourself. Just store in an airtight container out of the light.

— Serves 4 —

4 tablespoons vegetable oil

4 green cardamom pods

2 bay leaves

2 onions, finely chopped

1½ tablespoons ground coriander

1 teaspoon ground turmeric

2–3 teaspoons mild curry powder

1 heaped tablespoon plain flour

500ml chicken stock or water

8 skinless, boneless chicken thighs

3 tablespoons natural yogurt

a big pinch of sea salt

a big pinch of saffron

a handful of flat-leaf parsley, chopped

2 teaspoons garam masala (see below)

For the garam masala	*To serve*
1 tablespoon green cardamon pods, husks cracked	steamed or boiled basmati rice
1½ cinnamon sticks	½ cucumber, peeled and diced
½ teaspoon cloves	2 tomatoes, skinned, destalked and finely diced
1 teaspoon cumin seeds	4 tablespoons natural yoghurt
1 teaspoon coriander seeds	8 poppadoms
	3 tablespoons mango chutney
	2 shallots, sliced and fried in oil until brown and crisp, then drained on kitchen paper

To make your own garam masala, dry roast all the ingredients in a heavy-based pan over a medium heat until you smell the oils being released. Put into a spice grinder, grind, then store in an airtight container.

For the curry, heat the oil in a large pan, then add the cardamom pods and bay leaves, and cook until they crackle and pop. Add the onions and cook for about 15 minutes until soft, then add the ground coriander, turmeric and curry powder, plus the flour, and stir well.

Add the stock gradually, stirring to make a sauce, then add the chicken, yogurt, salt and saffron. Simmer gently for 20–25 minutes until the chicken is cooked through.

Stir in the parsley and garam masala, and cook for a couple more minutes, then retrieve the cardamon pods and bay leaves and discard.

Serve with basmati rice and other accompaniments.

Francatelli's Chicken à l'Indienne, George V's Curry and Elizabeth II's Curry (clockwise from top left)

George V's Curry

'King George V had far simpler tastes than his father,' writes Tschumi, 'and we had heard that as Prince of Wales he had shown little interest in any kind of food, except curry and Bombay duck, of which he was extremely fond, for the King had developed a taste for it in India.' It was not served when he had guests, but the King 'made it quite clear to M. Cedard [his head chef] that he did not see why it should not be provided for him at private luncheons. We made it from meat, game or chicken, depending what meat was available, but the King's favourite curry was one made from beefsteak and served with Bombay duck.' Bombay duck is a particularly ugly species of lizard fish, pink, with a great gaping mouth, eaten fresh, or sun-dried and salted. Hugely popular in Parsi and Bengali cuisine, as well as Gujarati, in coastal Maharashtra, Goa and Karnataka, along with Sri Lanka and Bangladesh, it's cooked into stews, curries, gravies, bhajis and chutneys. You can buy it online.

— Serves 4 —

8 chicken thighs, on or off the bone (Tschumi also used rabbit or pheasant, and you could use stewing beef too, a favourite of George V)

100g butter

3 large onions, chopped

1 garlic clove, crushed

2 cooking apples, peeled, cored and chopped

8 large tomatoes, skinned, deseeded and chopped

3 tablespoons curry powder

1 tablespoon chilli powder

1 bay leaf

1 litre good chicken stock

100g desiccated coconut

juice of 1 lemon

100ml double cream

To serve

steamed white basmati rice

dried, fried Bombay duck, crumbled (optional)

chopped fresh coriander (optional)

In a heavy casserole dish, brown the chicken in half of the butter. Remove from the pot and set aside.

Add the remaining butter to the casserole dish and gently fry the onions, then the garlic, then the apples and finally the tomatoes, until cooked but not browned. Mix in the curry and chilli powder.

Meanwhile, put the bay leaf, stock and coconut in a separate pan and bring to the boil. Strain the stock and add to the casserole. Cook for a further 10 minutes.

Add the chicken to the sauce and simmer gently for 45 minutes. Remove the chicken and set aside. If the sauce is still too thin, reduce further.

Pass the sauce through a sieve and return to the pot, then add the lemon juice and the cream. Simmer until it reaches a 'good thickness', then add the chicken back in. Simmer over a low heat for 10 minutes.

Serve with white basmati rice and Bombay duck and coriander, if using.

Francatelli's Chicken à l'Indienne

This is a Frenchman's take on an Indian curry. But not one eaten by Queen Victoria herself because hers were, according to Tschumi, 'the special province of her Indian cooks and servant', who killed their own sheep and poultry for the curries for 'religious reasons', as well as grinding their own curry powder between two large round stones and preparing their own spices. The curries were always served by 'two Indians in the showy gold-and-blue uniforms worn at lunchtime'. But when her son, Edward VII, ascended to the throne, he dispensed with their services, and curries were cooked in the royal kitchen. I've adapted this for the modern cook, replacing the 'cook's meat curry paste' with curry powder.

— Serves 4 —

8 skinless, boneless chicken thighs	1 blade of mace
100g butter	4 cloves
3 large onions, sliced	3 tablespoons medium curry powder
4 garlic cloves, chopped	1 teaspoon chilli powder
3 celery sticks, sliced	350ml chicken or vegetable stock

In a large sauté pan, fry the chicken pieces in half of the butter until they are browned all over. Remove from the pan and set aside.

Add the remaining butter to the same pan and gently cook the onions, garlic, celery, mace, cloves, curry and chilli powder until the vegetables are softened.

Add the stock, mix well, then return the chicken to the pan. Simmer gently for 45 minutes, or until the chicken is cooked through, before serving.

Duck with Stewed Peas

The original recipe uses duckling, slowly stewed, and was a Francatelli favourite, often on his menus for Queen Victoria. But I've borrowed Mark Hix's recipe, because I love the way the richness of the confit duck goes with the sweetness of the peas.

— Serves 4 —

4 duck legs

250g duck fat

4 garlic cloves, unpeeled

10 black peppercorns

5 cloves

1 bay leaf

2 teaspoons sea salt

1 large baking potato, cut into 4 slices about 1–2cm thick

For the peas

150g peas (shelled weight)

1 teaspoon caster sugar

grated zest and juice of 1 small orange

a handful of pea tendrils (pea shoots) or small salad leaves

salt

Preheat the oven to 180°C/350°F/gas mark 4. With a heavy, knife, chop the knuckle off the duck legs, then cut around the thigh bone with the point of the knife, ensuring you don't go through the skin, and chop the bone just below the knuckle. Fold the thigh in and push the drumstick meat down to expose the bone so each looks like a little ham. Pack the legs into a tight-fitting pan, then add the duck fat, garlic, peppercorns, cloves and bay leaf. Season well with salt, then cover the pan with a lid and cook in the oven for 1 hour, or until the legs are soft but not falling apart.

Turn the oven up to 200°C/400°F/gas mark 6. Lay the potato slices in an ovenproof pan, remove the duck legs from the fat and place one leg on top of each slice of potato. (You can strain the excess duck fat into an airtight container and keep it in the fridge to use at a later date.) Cook the potato and duck legs in the oven for about 30–35 minutes until the fat is crisp. You may want to put a little foil on the leg bones to prevent them from burning.

Meanwhile, cook the peas in boiling salted water with a teaspoon of sugar for 4–5 minutes until tender, then drain.

To make the dressing, put the orange zest and juice in a bowl and whisk in a tablespoon of the liquid duck fat.

To serve, remove the duck legs on their potato slices with a spatula or fish slice and transfer to serving plates. Arrange the stewed peas and pea tendrils or salad leaves around the duck and spoon around the dressing.

Shooting

'Shooting was certainly one of my father's greatest pleasures in life,' remembered the Duke of Windsor. 'For him the magic period from August to January meant glorious days on the moor, or "on the hill" in Scotland, or matching his skills with other famous "guns" during the partridge and pheasant seasons in England.' George V was one of the great shots of his era, as elegant as he was deadly. Although 'bags' (the term used to cover the number of birds shot) back then were notably excessive.

At the peak of the 'big shoots', in the years preceding the outbreak of the First World War, over 20,000 head of game were shot per year at Sandringham alone, while bags of 2,000 birds, shot by eight guns in a day, were not uncommon. Of course, every bird was picked, hung, plucked and devoured, with barely a scrap wasted. But these numbers were more slaughter than sport. Especially as the pheasants at Sandringham weren't exactly renowned for their speed or height.

Perhaps the bloodthirsty peak was reached in 1913, at Hall Barn, the home of Lord Burnham, owner of the *Daily Telegraph*. 'My father was deadly that day,' recalled David, his eldest son, 'and used three guns.' As the light faded, and the 'carnage' stopped, the bag was announced: 3,937 birds, and George had shot 1,000. Even he was troubled by the numbers. 'Perhaps we went a little too far today, David,' he said to his son on the drive back to London.

Thankfully, those days are long gone, and the rather awful spectacle of mass slaughter of unsporting birds is no longer considered acceptable. Quite right too. Shooting can only be justified if birds are killed cleanly. And eaten. Grouse is the first to appear on the menu, on the 'Glorious Twelfth' of August. When young, its flesh is sweet and elegant, softly scented with heather. Then partridge, from 1 September, the native English grey-leg birds possessing far more flavour than the 'Frenchies', or reared red legs. Pheasant season begins in October, while the peak of the deer-stalking season happens in October, too. All three game birds, along with venison, were very much the seasonal stars of every royal menu, from Victoria to the present day.

In fact, Balmoral was bought as a shooting estate by Prince Albert, who loved stalking deer. Shooting lunches at Sandringham, under Edward VII, took place in a field, within a vast tent, the floor swept and covered in straw. A royal standard fluttered above. Tables were clad in thick linen and formal crockery, while guests feasted upon mulligatawny soup, steak, kidney and lark pudding and roast pheasant. Lunches these days are a whole lot less extravagant: a chicken pie, perhaps, or Irish stew. And the shooting very much about conservation, the preservation of the countryside and supporting the rural economy, rather than obscenely senseless slaughter.

Partridge Hotpot

Mark Flanagan was Royal Chef to the late Queen and now to His Majesty King Charles III, and a very fine cook he is too. As well as having the patience of Job, he has an ability to stay cool under immense pressure, whether cooking a state banquet for 180 people, lunch for four or a diplomatic reception for 1,000. He's also an incredibly nice man. This recipe comes from *A Royal Cookbook: Seasonal Recipes from Buckingham Palace*, a book he wrote alongside Edward Griffiths. It makes use of the partridge, a game bird that comes into season at the start of September. Although the reared, red-legged partridge (or 'French') is more common, the far rarer, wild and native English grey leg has a better flavour.

— Serves 4 —

750g maincrop potatoes, peeled and sliced into 7.5mm slices

2–3 tablespoons vegetable oil

4 oven-ready partridges (if partridge is unavailable, poussins will do, or 8 boneless chicken thighs)

400g top-quality sausage meat

1 onion, diced

2 carrots, peeled and cut into 2cm pieces

2 leeks, trimmed and cut into 2cm pieces

150ml dry cider

3–4 sprigs of thyme

1 bay leaf

400–500ml game or chicken stock

25g butter

salt and freshly ground black pepper

Preheat the oven to 180°C/350°F/gas mark 4.

Parboil the sliced potatoes for 4–5 minutes in a large pan of lightly salted water until just tender but still holding their shape. Drain and leave to cool.

Heat 1 tablespoon of the oil in a heavy flameproof casserole dish over a medium heat. Season the partridges and fry for about 4 minutes, turning often, until golden brown all over. Transfer to a plate and set aside.

Roll the sausage meat into 12 neat balls, add to the hot pan and brown well all over, adding a little more oil, if needed. Remove from the pan and set aside with the partridges.

Add the onions, carrots and leeks with the remaining tablespoon of oil to the pan, reduce the heat and gently soften the vegetables without allowing them to gain too much colour for about 5 minutes, stirring often.

Meanwhile, cut the legs from the partridges and slice the breast meat away from the remaining bone (reserve the carcasses to make stock or soup). Pick out any visible shot.

Add the cider, thyme and bay leaf to the casserole, bring to the boil and then add 400ml of the stock. When the liquid has returned to the boil, add the partridge and sausage meat and season with salt and pepper. Add a little more stock, if needed, to just cover the meat.

Cover the mixture with overlapping slices of the parboiled potato and dot with the butter. Bake for 35–40 minutes until the potatoes are tender and golden brown.

Venison Stew

Game has always been central to royal food, and venison – along with grouse, partridge and pheasant – is a staple. This is a big, hearty sort of dish, served at shooting lunches and family lunches alike. Edward VII was a particular fan, as was his son, George V, and it was made using deer they had shot at Balmoral. If you don't have venison, beef will do.

— Serves 4 —

olive oil, for cooking

750g venison, diced

2 onions, diced

2 celery sticks, diced

2 carrots, peeled and diced

2 garlic cloves, finely chopped

1 tablespoon redcurrant jelly

300ml red wine

500ml beef stock

a good glug of Worcestershire sauce

1 bay leaf

1 teaspoon chopped thyme leaves

salt and freshly ground black pepper

mashed potato, to serve

Preheat the oven to 150°C/300°F/gas mark 2.

Heat a good glug of olive oil in a heavy casserole over a high heat and brown the venison in batches. Remove from the pan and set aside.

Add a little more oil to the pan, add the diced onion, celery and carrots, and cook over a medium heat for about 10 minutes, stirring often until soft and slightly coloured. Add the garlic and cook for another 2 minutes.

Increase the heat, add the redcurrant jelly and wine, and deglaze the pan, stirring until the boozy aroma has gone. Return the venison to the pan, add the stock, Worcestershire sauce and herbs, and season well with salt and pepper.

Bring to the boil, then cover and braise in the oven for about 3 hours, or until the meat is spoon-soft. Serve with mashed potato.

Scotch Broth

You can't go wrong with a Scotch broth. Simple, soothing and cheap to make, it shows that the tastes of the royal family could be resolutely down to earth. It was served regularly at Balmoral, from the reign of Queen Victoria onwards. This recipe comes from that Scottish genius, Jeremy Lee. I love his cooking as much as I love him.

— Serves 6 —

1kg lamb scrag end or neck fillet

50g pearl barley, rinsed

2–3 medium carrots, peeled and trimmed

2 medium onions

2 medium potatoes, peeled

1 swede, peeled and trimmed

200g baby turnips (if available), peeled and trimmed

3 leeks, cleaned and trimmed

1 small head cabbage

1 bay leaf and 1 sprig of thyme, tied with kitchen string

sea salt and freshly ground black pepper

Cut off any large chunks of fat on the meat. Place the meat in a large, heavy-based pot and cover with water. Bring to the boil and skim off any impurities that rise to the surface. Add more water to make up for that lost through evaporation and skimming, then return to the boil and reduce the heat to a simmer. Add the barley.

Cut the vegetables into small cubes, then add to the pot, starting with the carrots and finishing with the leeks and cabbage. Some fresh spring vegetables – new potatoes, peas, broad beans, et al – enhance the dish immeasurably, but these should be added to the pot no more than 20 minutes before serving. Add the herb bundle, season with salt and pepper, and let the broth tick away for 2 hours. Keep skimming any foam that rises to the surface.

It can be served right away, but tastes much better the next day.

Irish Stew

In March 1899, the soon-to-be Queen Mary departed for Nice to stay with Queen Victoria at Cimiez, 'sustained by Irish stew, which was made at Windsor and kept tepid by being wrapped in red flannel cushions.' It was also a shooting lunch staple from the reign of Edward VII onwards.

— Serves 4 —

2 middle necks of lamb, filleted, boned and bones reserved (you could also use shoulder or leg, but it does need to have some extra fat, as this is a slow-cooked dish)

900ml lamb stock (see Note in method)

700g carrots, peeled

450g floury potatoes (such as King Edward), peeled

450g waxy potatoes (such as Pentland Javelin or Maris Peer), peeled

1 onion, thickly sliced

a good pinch of fresh thyme leaves

salt and freshly ground black pepper

chopped fresh chives and flat-leaf parsley, to garnish

Cut the lamb into large chunks and put in a heavy-based saucepan. Traditionally, the meat is not browned. Pour in the stock and bring to the boil, skimming off all the impurities from the surface. Remove the pieces of lamb with a slotted spoon and reserve. Strain the stock through a fine sieve into a clean pan. Add the pieces of lamb back in and bring back to the boil, then reduce the heat, cover and simmer gently for 10 minutes.

Meanwhile, cut the carrots into pieces a little smaller than the pieces of lamb, and the potatoes into pieces the same size as the lamb. Add the carrots, floury potatoes and onion to the pan and simmer for 10 minutes. Next, add the waxy potatoes and the thyme and simmer for a further 15–20 minutes, or until the lamb is very tender. The floury potatoes will have broken down to thicken the sauce, while the waxy potatoes will have kept their shape.

Remove from the heat, cover and leave to stand, without stirring, for 15 minutes.

Check the seasoning, then serve sprinkled generously with chopped chives and parsley.

Note: Ask your butcher to bone the lamb for you, and have them give you the bones too. Make a well-flavoured stock using the bones and the trimmings from the carrots and onion, plus other vegetables and herbs you like.

Roast Rib of Beef

Roast rib of beef. As much an edible representation of England as it is stalwart of the Sunday lunch table. 'Oh! The Roast Beef of England, And old English Roast Beef,' roared Henry Fielding, novelist and author of *The Grub Street Opera*, his red-blooded paean to the joys of roasted meat and patriotism. 'When mighty Roast Beef was the Englishman's food, it ennobled our brains and enriched our blood.' And despite Edward VII's love of haute French cuisine, he also adored good old-fashioned English food. Roast beef with roast potatoes, Yorkshire puddings and lashings of gravy was a stalwart of the Sandringham table. And served every Sunday night at Buckingham Palace, too. Buy the best British beef you can afford, preferably from a good butcher. Rare breed beef can be wonderful, from Belted Galloway and White Park to Hereford and Aberdeen Angus, but producing amazing beef is so much more than just breed. It's a complex juggling act of feed, finishing, ageing and butchery. The production of great beef takes knowledge, experience and a lot of hard work.

— Serves 6 —

3–4kg rib of beef

2–3 tablespoons olive oil

a big glug of Worcestershire sauce

2 tablespoons English mustard powder

sea salt and freshly ground black pepper

Preheat the oven to 240°C/475°F/gas mark 9.

Massage the oil into the beef, then sprinkle with Worcestershire sauce, then mustard powder. Season lustily, then put into a roasting tin and into the oven. Roast for 20 minutes, then turn the oven down to 190°C/375°F/gas mark 5 and roast for another 10 minutes per 250g for rare.

Leave to rest in a warm place for 20 minutes before carving.

The Special Relationship

President Franklin D Roosevelt was a man who not only enjoyed his food, but knew its power, too. 'A gourmet with an instinct for people's hidden motivations,' wrote historian Alex Prud'Homme, 'FDR researched what his guests liked to eat, drink and smoke, then constructed a menu that was more than a simple list of things to eat. It was a meal layered with signs and symbols.' One morning in 1938, he read about a planned visit by George VI and Queen Elizabeth to Canada. Ostensibly a goodwill Commonwealth tour, there was a more important ulterior motive – to galvanise support against the rise of Nazi Germany.

FDR had seen Hitler's threat from afar, but the USA had little appetite for getting involved in another, expensive far-off war. Especially one supporting the British, whom many Americans still resented. But if FDR could persuade the King and Queen to visit the USA, then perhaps public opinion would soften. He wrote to the King, asking them for 'three or four days of very simple country life at Hyde Park [the Roosevelts' home in upstate New York] – an opportunity to get a bit of rest and relaxation'. The King accepted his invitation.

Despite successful visits by Edward VII and the Duke of Windsor (both as Prince of Wales), this was the first time a reigning British sovereign had set foot in the USA. And so in June 1939, the King and Queen found themselves sitting on folding chairs at Hyde Park, eating hot dogs served on silver platters. The King seemed a little nonplussed. 'What should I do?' he asked the President. 'Put it in your mouth and keep chewing until you finish it,' came the smiling response. 'King Tries Hot Dog And Asks For More,' cried the headline of *The New York Times*. 'And He Drinks Beer With Them.' The American public were delighted, seeing the royal couple as homely and down-to-earth, rather than frosty, former imperial overlords. Behind the scenes, the King and FDR discussed the Nazi threat, with the President promising to defend British Atlantic convoys, and sink German U-boats. In 1941, Roosevelt sent his troops into battle. That lunch became known as the 'picnic that won the war'.

Queen Elizabeth II made four official state visits over her reign, to Presidents Dwight D Eisenhower, Gerald Ford (New England lobster, stuffed saddle of veal), George Bush (Maine lobster, crown roast of lamb) and George W Bush (pea soup, Dover sole, saddle of spring lamb). But it was her relationship with President Reagan, with their shared love of horses, that was the warmest. Her trip to the Reagans' Rancho del Cielo, just outside Santa Barbara, California, in March 1981 was drenched in torrential rain more suited to Scotland than the West Coast. They ate enchiladas, chile rellenos, refried beans and guacamole. Quite what Her Majesty thought of her vibrantly spiced lunch, we'll never know. But one thing is for certain. Whatever her view, she would have pronounced it 'delicious'.

FDR's Hot Dogs

These are the hotdogs that played a starring role in 'the picnic that won the war' (see previous page). And while I'd never dare, as an Englishman, to wade into the debate as to the superiority of New York (steamed onions, mild mustard) over Chicago (chopped raw onion, yellow mustard, green relish, a dill pickle spear, peppers and celery salt) or Washington (half smoked dog, chili, mustard and onions), I do prefer raw onion to cooked.

— Serves 4 —

8 frankfurters (the best you can find – apparently, FDR served a local brand: Swishers)

8 hot dog buns

To serve

ketchup

mustard

chopped raw or fried onions (optional)

Bring a pan of water to the boil, then simmer the frankfurters for 3 minutes. Drain on kitchen paper.

Split and toast the buns, add the frankfurters and top with your condiments of choice.

Quiche de Lorraine

There have been endless egregious sins committed in the name of this French regional classic. Most of them by supermarkets, with their sullen frisbees of fridge-cold, inedibly sorry stodge – the very definition of drab dyspepsia. Elizabeth David once described the quiche as a 'culinary dustbin', and a quick glance at some of the more appalling versions – with tinned salmon or asparagus tips, shrivelled mushrooms and sweaty, processed ham – prove her point. There was even a tongue-in-cheek Eighties bestseller, called *Real Men Don't Eat Quiche*. But proper Quiche Lorraine – a glorious combination of crisp pastry, and wobbling, just-set custard, studded with crisp shards of smoky bacon – is something we all can love, a markedly superior tart. It featured quite heavily on the royal menus, but more as a savoury, a dish eaten between the main course and pudding. Tschumi has a recipe that is described as 'The Duchess of Gloucester's Savoury', but it's very much a bite-sized delight, and omits the bacon. This recipe is taken from the late, great Keith Floyd. He may not have been French, but red Burgundy certainly pulsed through his veins. His version is particularly purist, omitting even the Gruyère. Feel free to throw a generous handful into the egg and cream mix.

— Serves 4–6 —

200g plain flour, plus extra for dusting

100g unsalted butter, chilled and diced, plus 2 teaspoons extra for baking

3 tablespoons ice-cold water, or as needed

1 teaspoon white wine vinegar or lemon juice

150g smoked bacon, diced

4 large eggs, beaten

450ml double cream

salt and freshly ground black pepper

You will need

20cm fluted tart tin with a removeable base

baking beans

To make the pastry, tip the flour into a bowl and add the 100g cold, diced butter. Using your fingers, rub the butter into the flour until the texture is of fine sand with only small flecks of butter still remaining. Season well, then add the cold water and vinegar or lemon juice, and mix to combine using a round-bladed knife, adding more water if needed to bring the mixture together. Knead lightly to gather the dough into a ball, flatten into a disc, cover and chill for 1 hour.

Lightly dust the work surface with flour, roll out the pastry and use it to line the tart tin. Prick the bottom all over with a fork and chill again while you preheat the oven to 190°C/375°F/gas mark 5.

Line the pastry case with foil, fill with baking beans and blind bake for 20 minutes. Remove the foil and beans, and cook for a further 2–3 minutes to dry out the base.

Meanwhile, fry the bacon until crisp, remove from the pan and leave to drain on kitchen paper. In a bowl, beat together the eggs and cream, and season well with salt and pepper.

Increase the oven temperature to 200°C/400°F/gas mark 6. Place the tart tin on a baking tray, then sprinkle the bacon into the tart shell, pour over the eggs and cream and dot the top with little pieces of the extra 2 teaspoons of butter. Bake for a further 25 minutes until golden brown and set.

Serve warm or at room temperature.

Tea

Tea

Tea, that most British of mid-afternoon pursuits. Not the drink, although that plays a central role. But the one royal constant, that has barely changed from the days of Victoria. Who was a particular fan, thanks to her not being allowed to partake growing up, save as a 'great treat' in teenage years. Despite not having a sweet tooth, I love a proper tea. Sandwiches, crusts cut off, spread thick with butter and filled with slices of good ham, heavy on the mustard; smoked salmon, egg salad and roast beef. There are crumpets, hot and dripping with more butter, lavished with Marmite or honey. And cakes of every hue and flavour. British food may get an international (and totally unwarranted) kicking, but no one can argue the eternal appeal of a proper tea.

Victoria, according to a courtier, had a 'strong weakness for afternoon tea'. Even when out on the Scottish moors, John Brown and the other ghillies would boil a kettle in some 'sheltered corner', while the Queen and young princesses sketched. 'This refreshing cup of tea has ever ranked high in the Royal favour.' The confectionery cooks at Windsor were kept busy all year, since their role was 'principally to supply the Queen's tea table'. Her favourites included 'chocolate sponges, plain sponges, wafers of two or three different shapes, langues de chat, biscuits and drop cakes of all kinds, tablets, petits fours, princess and rice cakes, pralines, almond sweets and a large quantity of mixed sweets'. So much for that delicate appetite.

Little wonder she had quite the reputation as a lover of cake. 'It is known that the Queen of England eats macaroon cakes continually,' wrote the poet Edward Lear, who had once taught her drawing, 'and she also insists on her suite doing the same.' After devouring two scones, two pieces of toast and a few biscuits, she commented to Lady Lytton, in 1897, 'I'm afraid I must not have any more.' Such restraint was not the norm. According to her granddaughter, Princess Maud of Wales, she even dunked her cake in tea, in the German style. And would 'take tea' at the summerhouse, Adelaide Cottage or Swiss Cottage at Windsor, writing in her journals that she 'found' or 'took' tea which, as Annie Gray points out, was 'something of an over-simplification of what was often quite a convoluted process with a fair degree of planning and catering involved'.

Served at five on the dot, it was (and still is) the most relaxed of royal meals, a time for Edwardian (if not Victorian) women to remove their uncomfortable, tightly laced corsets, and slip into a tea dress, loosely fastened. This was the time when the patisserie chefs could really flex their culinary muscles, with eclairs, Chelsea buns, financiers, pralines and cakes, from lemon to chocolate and fruit. At Sandringham, Edward VII would appear, dressed in a short black jacket and black tie. And, accompanied by the merry tunes of his band, would dig into poached eggs, petit fours, rolls, cakes hot and cold, scones, preserved ginger (good for the digestion!) and 'that particular species of Scotch shortcake,' writes the historian Christopher Hibbert, 'of which he was especially fond.' Tea at the other palaces was equally expansive.

After the death of George V (another enthusiastic eater of tea), Queen Mary moved to Marlborough House, where she lived alone. Yet Gabriel Tschumi records how 'she abetted me in the business of providing cakes or biscuits for her young grandchildren'. On Monday 12 November 1951, she noted in her menu book, which was shared with the chef, that the Duke and Duchess of Gloucester would be coming to tea, along with their son, Prince Richard. The menu ran as follows: 'Bridge rolls aux oeufs et cresson. Sandwiches saumon fume; biscuits (home made); ginger cake; chocolate cake; sponge cake iced. Bread and butter.' The next day, the book returned, with messages alongside, written in her elegant hand. The smoked salmon sandwiches were deemed 'excellent'.

The late Queen also had a full afternoon tea every day. If it was just her and Prince Philip, there were always sandwiches, scones (never dressed), pastries and biscuits, both home-made and shop-bought, the Praline Choco-Leibniz being a favourite. As well as a large 'cutting' cake, a Genoise chocolate sponge, a Victoria sponge or Rich Tea chocolate biscuit cake.

With guests, at Balmoral or at Windsor, more savoury dishes would be added: potted shrimps, sardines on toast or a special tea purée, made from game, to be spread on toast. If children were coming, a special effort would be made to make things more fun.

In the case of Charles III and Queen Camilla, it's still a 5pm ritual, where we all gather together at a round table in the drawing room at Birkhall, after an afternoon spent outside, mushroom hunting. Or, in my case, buying second-hand cookbooks in nearby Ballater's brilliant Deeside Books.

There are always cakes, usually one chocolate and one fruit, along with flapjacks, occasional potted shrimps, crumpets in winter and, best of all, sandwiches. On a good day, I can put away a dozen. A good tea is a great thing. But an extra meal, however lovely, doesn't do wonders for the waist.

Afternoon Tea Sandwiches

Sandwiches are the highpoint of any serious tea, buttered lavishly, crusts cut off, and sliced into fat fingers. Don't stint on the filling. The Queen Mother's Mayonnaise would have been in constant use in the Queen Mother's kitchen, and is a recipe that I've adapted from a rather wonderful book called *The Royal Blue & Gold Cook Book*.

— All recipes make 6 finger sandwiches —

Smoked Salmon

50g salted butter, softened

4 slices of soft brown bread

100g good smoked salmon (Severn and Wye, Secret Smokehouse, John Ross and Daylesford are my favourites)

a generous squeeze of lemon juice

freshly ground black pepper

Butter the bread so the whole slices are coated. Layer salmon onto two of the slices, two slices thick. Squeeze over some lemon juice and grind over some black pepper. Place the second slices of bread on top, slice off the crusts and cut each sandwich into three fingers.

Ham & Mustard

50g salted butter, softened

4 slices of soft, white farmhouse bread

100g good-quality British ham (preferably York – the dry, proper stuff, not slimy, processed rubbish)

a big dollop of Colman's English mustard

Butter two slices of the bread so the whole slices are coated. Layer ham on top, two slices thick.

Spread a thin layer of mustard on each of the second slices of bread and place them on top, slice off the crusts and cut each sandwich into three fingers.

Egg Mayonnaise

50g salted butter, softened

4 slices of soft, white farmhouse bread

For the egg mayonnaise

4 eggs, added to boiling water and cooked for 8 minutes

3 tablespoons of the Queen Mother's Mayonnaise (or use shop-bought, if you must)

a couple of drops of Tabasco

a handful of chopped chives

a splash of white wine vinegar

a pinch of sea salt

a big screw of freshly ground black pepper

For the Queen Mother's Mayonnaise (makes about 600ml)

3 fresh egg yolks, at room temperature

1 teaspoon mustard

550ml vegetable oil

1–2 tablespoons white wine vinegar, mixed with a pinch of chopped tarragon

salt, to taste

To make the Queen Mother's Mayonnaise, beat the egg yolks with the salt and mustard until thick, and a lemon colour. Then gradually whisk in the oil and 1 tablespoon of vinegar, by droplets, into a creamy but firm mixture. It is very important to continue beating the sauce while adding the droplets of oil and vinegar. If using the mixer or blender, mix on high speed, being sure that all ingredients are well blended to achieve a thick substance. Once combined, add vinegar and salt to taste as the final step. This makes more than enough for sandwiches but will keep in the fridge in a sterilised jar for up to 2 weeks.

For the egg mayonnaise, peel the eggs, mash with a fork, then mix with the mayonnaise, Tabasco, chives, vinegar, salt and pepper.

Butter the bread so the whole of the slices are coated. Spoon 2 tablespoons of egg mayonnaise each on top of two of the slices, then place the second slices of bread on top. Slice off the crusts and cut each sandwich into three fingers.

Pictured overleaf

*Ham and Mustard,
Smoked Salmon, and
Egg Mayonnaise
Sandwiches (clockwise
from top left)*

Coronation Chicken Sandwiches

I know, I know, it really wouldn't be a royal cookbook without this so-called regal 'classic', officially known as *Poulet Reine* Elizabeth. It was created in 1953 by Constance Spry and Rosemary Hume, and served at the late Queen's Coronation lunch. Now the original version, as below, is perfectly civilised, but as the years went on, all manner of base and vile things were done to this perfectly innocent recipe, adding almonds and sultanas, lashings of turmeric and God knows what else, until it became a banana-hued, sickly-sweet aberration, the abject filling for a thousand sorry service station sandwiches. Originally made with poached whole chicken, I've made things a little easier by using poached breast, and have left out the whipped cream. I've also replaced the apricot purée with mango chutney.

— Makes enough for 12 sandwiches —

2 chicken breasts	1 bay leaf
1 onion, chopped	juice of 1 lemon, or as needed
2 tablespoons olive oil	2 tablespoons mango chutney
2 teaspoons curry powder	300g mayonnaise
1 teaspoon tomato paste	8 slices of brown bread
100ml red wine	butter, for spreading
100ml water	salt and freshly ground black pepper

Put the chicken breasts in a pan of water, bring to the boil and simmer for 10–15 minutes, or until the juices run clear from the thickest part of the breast. Allow to cool, then shred.

Fry the onion in the olive oil, over a medium heat, for 10 minutes until soft, then add the curry powder and cook for 2 more minutes. Add the tomato paste, increase the heat, then add the wine and cook to burn off the booze. Add the water, bay leaf and lemon juice, and simmer gently for 10 minutes.

Remove from the heat and pass the sauce through a sieve. Allow to cool.

Once the sauce is cool, add the mango chutney and mayonnaise, and mix well. Season to taste and add more lemon juice, if needed.

Mix the chicken with the sauce.

Butter four of the bread slices, top each generously with the chicken mixture, then press the second slices down on top. Remove the crusts and cut each sandwich into three fat fingers.

Potted Shrimp

ON CRUMPETS

Potted shrimp is the most English of dishes. Tiny brown shrimp (and they are the only crustacean we call 'shrimp', rather than 'prawn') with the very sweetest of flavours are covered in butter spiced with mace, bay and cayenne pepper. Potting is an old preservation technique. At Buckingham Palace and Windsor, there was usually some form of potted meat, beef and chicken in particular, perfect for invalids and hearty eaters alike. This really is the simplest recipe, but if you can't be bothered to make your own, then the best brown potted shrimp come from Morecombe Bay, in Lancashire. You can also buy them readymade from the great Baxters. This is a dish I've eaten at Birkhall for tea, as well as for a starter at dinner too. Or just as a deeply civilised snack. Serve cold on brown toast, or melted, as below, onto hot crumpets.

— Serves 6 —

175g unsalted butter

1 teaspoon freshly ground black pepper

½ teaspoon ground cayenne pepper

½ teaspoon ground mace

1 small bay leaf

450g peeled brown shrimp

salt

To serve

6 crumpets, toasted

2 lemons, cut into wedges

You will need

6 ramekins

Melt the butter in a saucepan, then add the black pepper, cayenne pepper, mace and bay. Throw in the shrimp and stir to coat. Cook for a couple of minutes until warmed through, then remove from the heat. Remove the bay leaf and check the seasoning.

Divide the shrimp mixture among six ramekins and season with a little salt. The butter should cover the shrimps. Chill in the fridge until set.

Pile high onto hot crumpets and serve with a slice of lemon.

Picnics & Barbeques

'The Queen always had a passion for eating in the open air, and has retained her taste for so doing until the present day.' So wrote an anonymous courtier, who then went on to describe, somewhat breathlessly, how Queen Victoria once made a 'delightful luncheon' on the moors above Balmoral, consisting of 'warmed-up broth and potatoes which she helped boil herself'. With the 'help' of a servant or two, no doubt. Seminal moments in royal history aside, both Victoria and Albert were enthusiastic al fresco feasters. And rarely set forth on a walk, stroll, stalk or shoot without a wicker basket filled with flasks of tea and a couple of fortifying fruit cakes.

And it's at Balmoral that the picnic tradition continues to this day. The Queen Mother was a picnic maestro and, according to her biographer William Shawcross, 'nothing gave her more pleasure than picnics and they happened almost every day, rain, snow or shine.' The food was simple, but 'fun, especially the jam puff and cream pastries which would explode all over the faces of the uninitiated'.

The late Duke of Edinburgh was renowned as a barbeque master, and he designed all of his own kit, including a portable grill, with three different racks, that can be moved up and down, for absolute grilling precision. It is a work of barbeque art. As is his picnic trailer, made to be towed behind a Land Rover, with lots of different compartments for everything from spices and herbs to tools, plates and cutlery. Form and function. Everything has its exact place, and woe betide the poor guest who put the mustard and ketchup in the drawer meant for tongs. Edward VII had his own specially designed hotbox, used for transporting food from kitchen to shooting picnic. It was used for George V's visit to France during the First World War.

Prince Philip would have made a fine engineer, and chef too. 'The Duke was truly interested in food, and was a hugely talented cook,' Mark Flanagan told me. 'He was a genuine gourmet, but never a snob. It was all about the flavour, and it didn't need to be complicated or overly fussy. He was a very unfussy man.' At Balmoral, he'd suddenly appear in the kitchen, in search of that night's dinner. Well-hung venison, grouse, a sirloin of beef, or sausages. 'He would then have his own marinade, and always had a firm idea of what he wanted to cook that night. It was an honour and pleasure to work for him.' His youngest son Edward, now Duke of Edinburgh, has taken over barbeque duties, although from my own recent experience, Peter Phillips, son of the Princess Royal, has certainly inherited his grandfather's way with fire. Those Balmoral barbeques still burn bright.

Queen Mary's Cheese Biscuits

These are little savoury snacks, made of cheese rather than for cheese. And, as the title makes clear, a great favourite of the eponymous Queen.

— Makes about 20 —

100g Parmesan, grated

100g unsalted butter, plus extra for greasing

100g plain white flour

1 teaspoon mustard powder

1 tablespoon finely chopped fresh rosemary

Mix everything into a paste in a food processor, then knead for a minute. Form into a ball, wrap in clingfilm and place in the fridge to rest for 30 minutes.

Preheat the oven to 180°C/350°F/gas mark 4.

Remove the clingfilm and roll the dough out thinly. Cut into 5cm squares and place on a greased baking sheet.

Bake for about 20 minutes, or until crisp and golden but not too browned.

Cool on a wire rack. They will keep in an airtight container for up to 4 days.

Balmoral Shortbread

This recipe comes from *Royal Chef*, by Gabriel Tschumi. 'Queen Victoria had a little of this almost every day,' writes Tschumi. As did Edward VII. I have adapted it to the modern kitchen, seeing as most of us sadly don't possess vast cast-iron, solid-fuel cookers.

— Makes about 32 pieces —

225g unsalted butter, softened

110g caster sugar, plus a little extra to finish

350g plain flour, plus extra for dusting

You will need

5cm plain round cutter

Cream the butter and sugar together until pale and smooth. Add the flour and work in until smooth and thoroughly combined, but do not overmix or this will toughen the shortbread.

Turn the mixture out onto a lightly floured work surface and roll out to a thickness of 3–4mm. Cut into discs using the round pastry cutter, arrange the shortbread on lined baking sheets and prick with a fork. 'Shortbread was always pricked in the same way at Buckingham Palace, in a domino pattern with three rows of three dots', writes Tschumi.

Sprinkle with a little more sugar and allow to rest in the fridge for 20 minutes.

Meanwhile, preheat oven to 170°C/325°F/gas mark 3.

Bake the shortbreads for 15–18 minutes until golden. Allow to cool on a wire rack.

Welsh Teabread

This is a recipe from the kitchen of Charles III. It was served when the King (then Prince of Wales) was in Wales, but it is still popular at tea, wherever he may be.

— Serves 8 —

1 mug of sultanas

1 mug of raisins

a large pinch of mixed peel, finely chopped

1 mug of soft brown sugar

1 mug of strong Earl Grey or smoked black tea

1 egg, beaten

1½ mugs of self-raising flour (or as needed)

Mix the fruit, peel and sugar in a large mixing bowl. Pour the mug of tea over the mixture and leave to soak for a few hours.

Meanwhile, preheat the oven to 150°C/300°F/gas mark 2.

Mix the soaked mixture well and fold in the beaten egg, then fold in enough self-raising flour to make a soft batter.

Grease and line a 900g loaf tin with baking paper, then pour in the batter and bake for just over 1 hour, until an inserted skewer comes out clean.

Turn out onto a wire rack to cool. Serve on its own or slathered with butter. This will keep well in an airtight container for up to 5 days.

Burn O'Vat Rock Cakes

'These rock cakes are named after Burn O'Vat, a beauty spot close to Balmoral between Ballater and Aboyne,' writes Michael Sealey in *A Taste of Mey*. 'They were served to the Royal Family for teas and picnics in Scotland.'

— Makes 8 —

75g unsalted butter, plus extra for greasing

250g self-raising flour

75g golden granulated sugar

75g mixed dried fruit

25g mixed chopped peel

1 teaspoon mixed spice

1 egg, lightly beaten

2 tablespoons milk (or as needed)

demerara sugar, to decorate

Preheat the oven to 180°C/350°F/gas mark 4 and grease a baking sheet with butter.

Place the flour and sugar in a mixing bowl and rub in the butter until the mixture resembles sand. Add the mixed fruit, peel and spice, and stir into the sandy mixture. Add the egg and enough milk to bind the mixture to a rough, thick, doughy texture.

Using a dessertspoon, shape the mixture into rough ball shapes, then place on the prepared baking sheet and flatten slightly. Sprinkle with demerara sugar, then bake for about 25 minutes, or until firm and golden brown.

Turn out onto a wire rack to cool. Eat warm or at room temperature, ideally the same day.

Jam Puffs

These were firm favourites at the Queen Mother's hillside picnics at the Castle of Mey. But newcomers beware. There is definitely an art to eating them, and one that wasn't always made clear. As the Earl of Caithness remembers, 'I had to eat it in my fingers and firstly bite off a corner before pouring in the cream. I then had to eat it making as little mess as possible. There was a great deal of laughter from everyone else as the cream firstly ran out of my hands and then dripped on to whatever was below. I just hoped that a new guest would arrive soon to complete the challenge!' This recipe comes from Sue Collings, in *A Taste of Mey*.

— Makes 16 —

plain flour, for dusting

320g puff pastry

4–5 tablespoons jam or marmalade

1 egg, beaten

icing sugar, for dusting

double cream (optional), to serve

You will need

8cm plain round pastry cutter

Dust the work surface with flour and roll out the pastry to a thickness of no more than 2mm. Chill the pastry for 15 minutes, then stamp out 16 discs with the cutter (re-rolling the scraps as needed).

Spoon a scant teaspoon of jam in the centre of each pastry disc. Lightly brush around the jam with beaten egg, then fold the pastry in half to form a half moon. Use finger and thumb to press around the edges to seal, then use a fork to crimp the edges of each parcel. Do not prick the top as this will let the filling out.

Place on a lined baking sheet and chill for 15 minutes while you preheat the oven to 180°C/350°F/gas mark 4.

Bake on the middle shelf of the oven for about 15 minutes until golden brown.

Leave to cool, then lightly dust with icing sugar to serve with cream, if liked.

Food on an Ocean Wave

'The real test of a good chef,' noted Gabriel Tschumi, 'is whether or not he can prepare a ten-course royal meal on a small paddle steamer in rough weather, sharing the galley with a good many of the crew.' As magnificent as the interiors of *Victoria and Albert II* were, all thick Brussels carpet, plush banquettes and huge open fireplaces, the galley was pretty near hellish. Not only was it minute, and unbearably hot too, but the five-man brigade had to share their space with the ship's company cooks. 'Those slightly frayed tempers which resulted from these encounters made it difficult to concentrate on the preparation of a sauce or the making of a poulet Danoise.'

Things were a little better on *Victoria and Albert III*, launched in May 1899. With her vast, steam-powered engines and twin-screw propulsion, two yellow funnels and three towering masts, she was faster, and more comfortable, than her predecessor. She carried a crew of three hundred and a household staff of thirty. And although the galley had rather more space, cooking was done on coal ranges. With limited ventilation. 'You only had to turn your back for the wind to change,' said Tschumi, 'and unless you were very quick a soufflé or a lark pudding was soon ruined in a cold oven.' Conversely, when the fires were raging, the galley was as hot as Hades. On one occasion, Edward VII came down to visit. 'Phew! I'm glad that's over,' he muttered, as he emerged from the inferno, his face beet red and gleaming with sweat. He never ventured down there again.

Edward, of course, expected exactly the same high standards of cooking onboard as he did at any other royal residence, with up to twelve courses at both lunch and dinner. Lamb cutlets, roast grouse and dressed crabs for the Shah of Iran. Pea soup, baby sea bass, roast beef and asparagus for a summer lunch just off Venice. In contrast to his father, George V, who (despite being a fine sailor) liked neither rich food nor rough seas.

Britannia, though, who launched in April 1953, was perhaps the greatest yacht of them all. While the galley was by no means as capacious as the kitchens at Buckingham Palace, it could easily cater for a state banquet for fifty-six in the dining room. Food was prepared by the Buckingham Palace chefs, assisted by head navy cook 'Swampy' Marsh, and sent up two floors above via a lift. Menus would feature a drawing of Britannia, just as they had in Victoria and Edward's day. By the reign of Queen Elizabeth II, dinners rarely went beyond three courses. But the sleekly elegant majesty of *Britannia*, as she glided into ports across the world, cannot be underestimated. Not just a floating palace, but the true Sovereign of the Seas.

Ginger Cake

This recipe comes from Jamie Sutherland, who often sends cakes to Birkhall for the King and Queen. His ginger cake is a classic, with a good fiery kick.

— Serves 8 —

1 × 350g jar of stem ginger in syrup

300g plain flour

2–3 teaspoons ground ginger

1 teaspoon ground cinnamon

1 teaspoon mixed spice

a pinch of salt

155g unsalted butter

125g dark brown muscovado sugar

140g golden syrup

140g black treacle

250ml full-fat milk

1 heaped teaspoon bicarbonate of soda

2 large eggs, lightly beaten

You will need:

deep, 20cm round cake tin

Preheat the oven to 170°C/325°F/gas mark 3 and line the base and sides of the cake tin with baking paper.

Drain the stem ginger, reserving the syrup. Finely chop the ginger.

Sift the flour, spices and salt into a large mixing bowl and use a fork to give it a quick stir to make sure the ingredients are thoroughly combined.

Put the butter, sugar, syrup, treacle and 100g of the reserved ginger syrup into a medium saucepan and mix together over a low heat until the sugar has melted, stirring all the time. Remove from the heat and whisk in the milk, bicarbonate of soda and eggs.

Using an electric beater or balloon whisk, slowly add the butter and syrup mixture to the flour, mixing until thoroughly combined. The batter will be very wet. Add the chopped stem ginger.

Pour the batter into the prepared tin and bake for 1 hour until well risen, deep brown in colour and the middle is firm. A wooden skewer inserted into the middle of the cake should come out clean.

Remove from the oven and leave to cool for 15 minutes. Make holes over the top of the cake with a skewer and pour over any remaining ginger syrup. Leave the cake in the tin for 20 minutes, then cover a wire rack with a clean tea towel and turn the cake out onto it. Turn the cake the right way up and leave to cool completely.

Wrap the cake in foil or baking paper and store in an airtight container or cake tin for a day or two before cutting.

Two Recipes from Mildred Dorothy Nicholls

Mildred Dorothy Nicholls entered service at Buckingham Palace as 7th Kitchen Maid in 1908, and left in 1919, as 3rd Kitchen Maid. She left behind a handwritten book of recipes, which is kept in the Royal Archive at Windsor. There's something rather thrilling about primary sources like this: a direct link to the royal kitchens, a glimpse of real history. Her hand is mainly neat (but occasionally illegible), and her recipes precise, although, as is the case with people who cook every day, they can be a little vague. So I've added and modernised them somewhat. But she gives us a fascinating, and first-hand, insight into royal eating in the early 20th century.

Swiss Roll

The choice of jam is up to you, but do spread with a generous hand.

— Serves 6–8 —

butter, for greasing

plain flour, for dusting

6 eggs

225g caster sugar, plus extra for dusting

a pinch of salt

225g fresh fine white breadcrumbs

4–5 tablespoons good-quality jam

You will need

30 × 40cm Swiss roll tin

Preheat the oven to 180°C/350°F/gas mark 4. Grease and line the base and sides of the Swiss roll tin with buttered and floured baking paper.

Separate the eggs, placing the yolks in one large mixing bowl and the whites in another.

Whisk the yolks with the sugar for about 2 minutes using a handheld mixer until pale and the mixture holds a ribbon trail when the whisk is lifted from the bowl.

Use a clean whisk to beat the egg whites with a pinch of salt until they hold stiff peaks.

Mix the breadcrumbs into the yolks, then fold one-third of the egg whites into the breadcrumb mixture to lighten. Fold in the remaining egg whites in two batches.

Carefully pour the mixture into the prepared tin and spread level. Bake for about 15 minutes until set and golden.

Carefully flip the cake out of the tin onto a large sheet of baking paper that has been liberally dusted with caster sugar. Peel off the lining paper and spread the sponge with jam. Trim all four sides of the sponge, then score a line across the sponge about 2cm from one of the shorter edges (this should make the first roll of the sponge easier to do). With this short side closest to you, roll the cake into a tight spiral using the sugared paper to support the cake as you roll.

Slide onto a serving plate and leave to cool completely before cutting into slices to serve.

Ginger Nuts

Another recipe taken from royal kitchen maid Mildred Dorothy Nicholls' cookbook. A classic British biscuit, and incredibly easy to make too. Feel free to up the ginger if you want more bite.

— Makes 12 biscuits —

120g self-raising flour

2 teaspoons ground ginger

1 teaspoon bicarbonate of soda

50g granulated sugar

50g unsalted butter, at room temperature

50g golden syrup

Preheat the oven to 180°C/350°F/gas mark 4 and line a baking sheet with baking paper.

Sift the flour, ginger and bicarbonate of soda into a bowl, add the sugar and mix to combine. Add the butter in small pieces and rub in using your fingers, as if making a crumble topping.

Add the golden syrup and mix into a big sticky ball. Evenly divide the mixture into 12 pieces and roll into balls in your hands, each ball roughly the size of a walnut. Place on the baking tray and flatten a little with the heel of your hand. Leave a decent space between each biscuit to allow for spreading during cooking.

Bake for 10–12 minutes until firm and golden. Leave to cool on a wire rack.

Birkhall Scones

These scones are the star at many a teatime in the royal household, crisp on the outside, fluffy within. Best served split in half, with clotted cream and strawberry or raspberry jam made from fruit picked from the garden. As to what goes on first, I don't dare get involved, as the rivalry between Devon (cream first) and Cornwall (jam first) is as eternal as it is fierce. Oh, and it's scone like gone, not scone like cone.

— Makes 10 —

40g butter, plus extra for greasing

225g self-raising flour, plus extra for dusting

1 tablespoon caster sugar

150ml milk (or as needed)

To serve

clotted cream

jam

You will need

6cm plain round pastry cutter

Preheat the oven to 200°C/400°F/gas mark 6 and grease a baking sheet with butter.

Sift the flour into a mixing bowl, then add the butter and rub with fingertips until the mixture looks like fine breadcrumbs. Mix in the sugar, then add the milk (you may not need it all) and mix until a dough comes together. Try not to overwork the dough.

Tip the dough out onto a floured surface and roll out to a thickness of about 2.5–3cm. Cut out 10 discs with the floured cutter (re-rolling the scraps as needed). Place on the prepared baking sheet and brush the tops with the remaining milk.

Bake for 12 minutes, then turn out onto a wire rack to cool slightly (although they are wonderful served warm). They will keep for a day or so in an airtight container but should really be enjoyed as fresh as possible.

Queen Mary's Birthday Cake

Another recipe from Gabriel Tschumi. 'Queen Mary knew that young people liked cakes,' he wrote in his book, *Royal Chef*, 'so I made a point of providing a choice of three different kinds.' This one was served to a young Prince Richard (now Duke of Gloucester) during the 1951 visit that I mentioned at the start of this chapter (see page 101). Among her observations, the Queen had heavily underlined the chocolate cake, written Prince Richard's name and the words 'great success'. The famed cake was also served each year at Queen Mary's birthday.

— Serves 8 —

125g melted butter, plus extra for greasing

8 egg yolks

2 egg whites

200g golden caster sugar

200g self-raising flour, plus extra for dusting

For the chocolate ganache

600ml double cream

100g caster sugar

450g good-quality dark chocolate, grated

You will need

two 20cm round cake tins

Preheat the oven to 180°C/350°F/gas mark 4. Grease and flour the cake tins.

Whip the eggs and sugar in a bain marie (a heatproof bowl set over a pan of simmering water – do not let the base of the bowl touch the water) until thick and you reach the ribbon stage (the beaters when lifted will leave a ribbon trail of batter). Sift in the flour in three stages, gently folding in each time, then add the melted butter and fold in until incorporated.

Pour the batter into the prepared cake tins and bake in the oven for 30 minutes, or until an inserted skewer comes out clean. Remove from the oven to a wire rack to cool in the tins, then remove from the tins to cool completely.

For the ganache, combine the cream, sugar and chocolate in a heavy saucepan and bring to the boil, then leave for 1 hour to cool.

Cut each cake in half and spread each layer with ganache, building up to a four-layer sandwich. Coat the entire surface of the cake with the remaining ganache.

Iced Coffee

A Garden Party stalwart, served in both the royal and main tea tents alike. The key is to use good coffee (this is not the time for instant) and not make it TOO sweet.

— Serves 2 —

400ml coffee (made using either the drip method, cafetière or coffee machine)

50ml milk

50ml double cream

2 tablespoons demerara or brown sugar

3 handfuls of ice

Make the coffee and allow to cool, then add it to a blender along with milk, cream, sugar and ice. Blend until smooth and pour into two glasses.

Lemonade

The other Garden Party classic, this needs a good tart kick. The perfect refreshment, in blazing sun and soggy downpour alike.

— Makes 1 litre —

8 unwaxed lemons

120g white sugar

plenty of ice

1 litre sparkling mineral water, chilled

a few sprigs of mint

Squeeze the lemons into a jug, discarding any pips. Add the sugar and stir until completely dissolved, about 2–3 minutes.

Add lots of ice, then the sparkling mineral water, and stir for another minute.

Serve immediately, with a sprig of mint in each glass.

Dinner

Dinner

Dinner with Queen Victoria could be a fairly fraught affair. Not that one lacked sustenance. Far from it. With up to fourteen courses to battle through, choice was never an issue. But the monarch had little interest in appreciating every last bite, however exquisite. 'She eats too much, and almost always a little too fast,' griped her uncle, Leopold I of Belgium. The Whig politician Thomas Creevey agreed. 'She eats quite as heartily as she laughs,' he noted of the young Queen in 1837. 'I think I may say she gobbles.'

Which would all be well and good. But royal etiquette demanded that as soon as the monarch had laid down her gilded knife and fork the rest of the table had to follow. And even if you were only part way through your *pojarski de volaille*, the plate would be whisked away, to be replaced by the next course. Well, towards the end of the Queen's reign anyway, when service *à la russe* (where one course was served, individually after another) had replaced service *à la française* (where dishes were all placed on the table together for guests to help themselves). Most supping at the royal table accepted this without so much as a mutter. But Lord Hartington, politician and future Duke of Devonshire, was made of sterner stuff. 'Here, bring that back,' he bellowed to a 'scarlet-clad marauder'. Silence fell over the room, and all eyes turned towards the sovereign. For once, thankfully, Her Majesty was amused.

After a mighty breakfast and heroic lunch, dinner really was the epicurean (or dyspeptic) summit of the day. It would always start with soup, followed by *poissons*, *entrées*, *relevés* (or 'removes', a mixture of roast meat and more elaborate dishes), and *rôtis* (more roast, but usually of smaller birds), then sometimes, as part of a state banquet, another *relevé* course (generally something sweet or a savoury), eventually ending with *entremets* (various vegetables, small savoury dishes and puddings). And the ubiquitous side table of cold joints.

Even on a night at the opera, Edward VII had a ten-course cold feast of lobster salad, various roast beasts and birds, as well as numerous puddings, laid out in his private room, behind the royal box. All served on gold plates, crisp linen and scented by vast bunches of flowers. At 9.30pm, the King and his guests would tuck in. Before waddling back in for the second half.

By the reign of George VI, things were rather less extravagant. Second World War rationing put an end to excess (which had been slowly melting away since the reign of George V), and tastes had changed too. 'It would be naïve to imagine that royalty always dine off rare delicacies,' wrote Alma McKee, cook to both Elizabeth II and the Queen Mother. 'Now it is only on rare occasions that the Royal family have five courses. Usually, it is not more than three and the food is good but simple.' Some gravadlax, perhaps (McKee was Swedish), then fish cakes. With brown-bread ice cream for pudding.

State banquets, though, remain one last link to those great feasts of old – formal, ornate and a gentle reminder of the power of soft, or 'soufflé', diplomacy. There may be rather fewer courses these days, but this is entertaining on the most magnificent scale. Presidents and prime ministers, emperors and shahs, kings, queens and princes. And powerful not so much for what is said (no discussions of policy here), rather for what they represent – continuity, ceremony, stability and the communal power of the shared table. People brought together by food. Albeit at the most elevated level. No politics or partisanship, no Machiavellian machinations (that's left to the courtiers) – rather, edible statecraft, pure dinnertime diplomacy.

Menus are still written in French and sent up for the sovereign's approval. When Mark Flanagan was cooking for the late Queen, he would offer her a choice of five. Highly spiced food was not an option, nor garlic or bivalves. Seasonality was as important as ever, with as many ingredients as possible harvested from the royal estates. 'Her Majesty always designed the menus for her guests, rather than herself,' he told me. 'And added her own suggestions, or remembered that so-and-so really liked this or that the last time they came. Her memory was incredible. All the menus had her hand on them.'

State banquets are held up to three times per year, at either St George's Hall at Windsor (where the table, made in 1846, is 53 metres long and can fit up to 160 guests) or in the ballroom at Buckingham Palace, where a large, horseshoe-shaped table is set up, with the King and the visiting head of state sitting at its centre. The whole evening glides and flows like a beautifully choreographed ballet. Flowers bloom, gold glitters and glasses, six per person, gleam.

The relationship between head chef and palace steward is all important. Red and green traffic lights are hidden in the balustrades of the far balcony of the Buckingham Palace ballroom. When the lights change, one course is removed and the next brought in. At St George's Hall, finished dishes are carried out in hot trolleys, most sent up in a small, two-person lift. The rest goes up the stairs with the footmen, scurrying up and down in full livery, 'like red-coated ants'.

In contrast to all the pomp of a state banquet is a private dinner at home, be it at Clarence House, Windsor, Highgrove or Birkhall. Soup, an omelette and a glass of wine. Sometimes, simplicity is the greatest luxury of all.

A Martini Fit for a King

The regal martini is most definitely stirred, not shaken.

— Serves 1 —

lots of ice

⅔ small wine glass of gin,
about 120ml

1 capful of Martini

1 wedge of lime

Put the ice in a glass and splash in the gin. Add the Martini, then squeeze in the lime, putting the squeezed fruit into the cocktail. Stir vigorously with a finger and drink.

Les Petits Vol-au-Vents

À LA BÉCHAMEL

Ah, vol-au-vents, the frilly-edged punchline of many a stale gastronomic joke. But this is a dish more sinned against than sinning, a once mighty mouthful brought low by grim, greasy, margarine-infected pastry with a filling that resembles cat sick. But enough of that. Because a vol-au-vent, well made, is a glorious thing, all buttery, flaky puff, filled with ham, or prawns, or poached chicken, enveloped in the most creamy of béchamel sauces. They pop up on royal menus from Queen Victoria onwards, as both entrée and savoury. And seem to be having their time in the sun once more, in some of the more modish of London restaurants. Francatelli has a recipe for *Vol-au-Vent à la Nesle*, which involves calf's brains, sweetbreads, quenelles of fowl, truffles, cocks' combs and *sauce Allemande*. Sounds divine, but this recipe is a touch more simple. You can, of course, make your own puff pastry, but a good frozen, butter-based ready-made will do the job. And feel free to substitute the chopped ham for anything else you like. The remains of the previous day's turbot was a particular favourite of Victoria's, although smoked haddock would do just fine.

— Serves 4, as a snack or starter —

4 large vol-au-vent cases, either homemade or bought ready-made

1 egg, lightly beaten

40g butter

30g plain flour

600ml full-fat milk

1 teaspoon English mustard powder

a pinch of cayenne pepper

50g button mushrooms, sliced

2 × 2.5cm-thick slices of good ham, chopped to a small dice

a large pinch of chopped fresh parsley, to serve (optional)

salt and freshly ground black pepper

Preheat the oven to 180°C/350°F/gas mark 4.

Glaze the vol-au-vent cases with the beaten egg, then bake for about 20 minutes, or according to the packet instructions.

Melt 30g of the butter in a saucepan, then gradually stir in the flour until smooth. Slowly add the milk, whisking and adding more as the sauce thickens. Simmer for 5 minutes, then add the mustard powder and cayenne pepper, and season with salt and pepper.

In a separate pan, cook the mushrooms in the remaining 10g of butter until soft, about 5 minutes. Add the diced ham and heat through, then add the mixture to the béchamel sauce.

Fill the pastry shells with the sauce and sprinkle with chopped parsley, if using, to serve.

Artichokes à la Barigoule

Served to Queen Victoria by her chef, Charles Elmé Francatelli, at Buckingham Palace on 24 October 1841, this is a sun-drenched, Provençal classic. And a regular on palace menus. The name comes, incidentally, from the Provençal word for thyme, *farigoule*, although others claim it refers to the barigoule mushroom, originally used, they say, to stuff it. Small, young artichokes are best, but the bigger ones are easier to get hold of.

— Serves 4 —

4 large artichokes or 12 small ones

1 bowl of water with the juice of ½ lemon

3 tablespoons olive oil

50g smoked lardons

1 small onion, sliced

3 garlic cloves, sliced

a big pinch of fresh thyme, leaves stripped from stalk and finely chopped

150ml dry white wine

150ml chicken stock

salt and freshly ground black pepper

First, prepare your artichokes. If using big ones, strip off all the leaves until you reach the pale, thin ones that surround the heart. Cut off the stalk about 1cm from the bottom of the heart, then remove the rest of the leaves, cutting carefully around the heart to remove any more green bits, but careful not to cut into the heart. Use a teaspoon to scrape out all the fibrous choke. For baby artichokes (with no choke), remove the first two rows of green leaves, then chop off the tips of those remaining. Trim the stalk. Put the trimmed artichokes in the bowl of lemon water, to stop them going brown.

Heat the oil in a heavy-based casserole with a lid and fry the lardons until crisp. Remove and set aside.

Add the onions to the same oil and sweat over a low-medium heat for about 15 minutes, then add the garlic and thyme, and cook for a further 5 minutes. Turn up the heat, add the white wine and cook to burn off the booze, about 2 minutes. Add the stock and season with salt and pepper.

Add the artichokes to the pot, stalks down, bring to a simmer and cover with the lid. The big artichokes will take 45 minutes–1 hour (use a sharp knife to check if done through), the smaller 30–45 minutes. If the liquid starts to reduce too quickly, add some boiling water.

When done, remove the artichokes to a warm plate. Strain the sauce through a sieve and pour it over the top. Sprinkle with the crisp lardons and serve.

Broad Beans à la Crème

Nothing announces the start of summer like broad beans, preferably the size of your small fingernail, blanched, then slathered in butter. When they get a little older, it's best to pop those vividly green kidneys from the tough outer shell. A hassle, but one that is very much worth your while. This recipe is adapted from Francatelli. I've cut down the cooking times, otherwise you'd end up with a green mush, and reduced some of the more extreme Victorian dairy excess.

— Serves 4 as a side —

500g fresh broad beans, shelled (and popped from skins if too big)

100g butter

a pinch of ground nutmeg

100ml double cream

6 slices of streaky smoked bacon, cooked until crisp

salt and freshly ground black pepper

1 tablespoon chopped parsley, to serve

Blanch the broad beans in boiling water for no more than 30 seconds. Drain.

Heat the butter in a large frying pan until foaming, add the broad beans, seasoning and nutmeg, and cook for a minute. Add the cream and cook for a further 2 minutes.

Crumble the bacon and parsley over the top and serve.

Mushrooms à la Crème

Charles Oliver grew up in the Royal Household under Queen Victoria, left to fight in World War I, was seriously injured at Gallipoli, but recovered and returned to royal service, under the then Prince of Wales, briefly Edward VIII. He died in 1965, leaving behind a mass of menus, recipes and anecdotes. He stipulated that they could only be published after his death. They were, and the book was named *Dinner at Buckingham Palace*. Prince Philip was a very keen cook and Oliver says he travelled everywhere with his 'electric, glass-covered frying pan.' He also cooked for Queen Elizabeth II, once the servants had been dismissed, usually classic nursery food such as scrambled eggs and smoked haddock, Scotch woodcock, and this mushroom dish.

— Serves 4 as a side —

500g mushrooms (field or button)
50g butter
1 teaspoon plain flour
200ml double cream
a squeeze of lemon juice
salt and freshly ground black pepper

croutons or brown toast, to serve (see below)

For the croutons
2 slices white bread, crusts removed
3 tablespoons sunflower oil
flaky sea salt

Clean and trim the mushrooms and chop into halves or quarters if large.

In a large frying pan, heat the butter until foaming over a medium-high heat. Add the mushrooms and cook for about 5 minutes, stirring often, until tender.

Sprinkle in the flour, season well and stir to combine. Reduce the heat slightly, add the cream, mix well and cook for 2 minutes until the mushrooms are soft. Add a squeeze of lemon juice and then serve either scattered with fried croutons or on toast.

Note: If making your own croutons, cut the bread into small cubes. Heat the oil in a frying pan over a medium heat, add the cubed bread and fry until crisp and golden brown, stirring almost constantly. Drain on kitchen paper and sprinkle with salt.

Pictured on previous page

Queen Camilla's Scrambled Eggs

Another favourite growing up, my mother, Queen Camilla, seemed to be able to make huge quantities of these, with the minimum of fuss. It was also a Boxing Day staple – some (relatively) light relief, usually made with our own eggs, that always seem to taste better than any other on earth. My father still keeps chickens, which he feeds on scraps, and which scratch about happily all day long. I've never eaten a finer egg. Princess Margaret didn't like the word 'scrambled' and insisted on calling them 'buttered eggs', which certainly has an appealing burr. The key to this is cooking over a very low heat. My mother does it on top of the Aga, the pan (which needs to be quite big) half off the coolest hotplate. Serve on hot buttered brown toast with a few slices of smoked salmon, if the urge takes you.

— Serves 2 —

4 eggs

a pinch of sea salt

a few screws of black pepper, plus extra to serve

30g salted butter

smoked salmon slices, to serve (optional)

2 thick slices of brown bread, toasted and buttered

Beat the eggs with the salt and pepper, but not too roughly – just ensure they're well mixed.

Melt the butter in a large frying pan until it starts to foam, then add the eggs. Stir with a wooden spoon over a very low heat. If the crust on the bottom appears too quickly, remove from the heat. You want thick, creamy curds, rather than that awful, overcooked mess with the texture of wall insulator. This will take any time between 10 to 20 minutes.

When almost done, but still runny, remove from the heat. Put some smoked salmon (if using) on buttered toast and spoon the eggs over the top with some extra black pepper.

Do NOT add a garnish of curly parsley.

Green Omelette

A dish I've eaten at Birkhall and Highgrove many times, this is a take on *Omelette aux Fines Herbes*, with the addition of Gruyère and mushrooms. The key is to keep the outside burnished, while the centre oozes gently.

— Serves 1 —

150g mushrooms (ceps have the best flavour), sliced

50g butter

3 Burford Brown eggs plus 1 yolk

½ teaspoon English mustard

½ teaspoon Dijon mustard

5g flat-leaf parsley, freshly chopped

6g tarragon, freshly chopped

neutral oil, for frying

80g Gruyère cheese, grated

salt and freshly ground black pepper

Sauté the mushrooms in the butter until nearly crispy and set aside.

Whisk together the eggs and egg yolk, add the mustards and season with some salt and pepper. Stir in the chopped herbs.

Heat a non-stick frying pan. Once hot, drizzle in a little oil and pour in the egg mixture. Cook, stirring continously, for around 1 minute, then stop stirring and allow the base to set.

Sprinkle the grated cheese and crispy mushrooms on top of the eggs, carefully fold the omelette over onto a serving platter and serve.

Oeufs en Meurette

'The King is partial to an egg in the first course of dinner,' remembers food writer Matthew Fort, who kindly provided this recipe. 'As I discovered the first time I cooked for him in Romania. This posed a logistical challenge in that the kitchen I had to work in wasn't exactly equipped with the last word in culinary technology. I came up with *Oeufs en Meurette* the second dinner I cooked for him. It's a fine, rollicking Burgundian classic (actually a variation on *Oeufs à la Bourguignonne*) and had the advantage that I could prepare all the elements except poaching the eggs in advance. It seemed to go down quite well.'

— Serves 4 —

350ml robust red wine

225ml beef or veal stock

1 onion

1 carrot

2 shallots

1 celery stick

2 small garlic cloves, crushed

bouquet garni of thyme, bay leaf and parsley

6 black peppercorns

3 tablespoons olive oil

85g unsmoked bacon lardons

20g plus 2 teaspoons butter

100g button mushrooms, halved if large

12 pearl onions, peeled

2 teaspoons plain flour

4 eggs

4 × 5mm-thick slices of baguette

salt and freshly ground black pepper

chopped parsley or chervil, to garnish

Pour the wine and stock into a saucepan. Roughly dice the onion, carrot, shallots and celery, and add to the pan with the garlic, bouquet garni and peppercorns. Bring to the boil over a medium heat and continue to boil for 15–20 minutes until the wine and stock have reduced by half. Strain into a clean pan through a fine-mesh sieve, pressing the vegetables with the back of a spoon to extract as much flavour as possible. Set aside.

Heat 1 tablespoon of the olive oil in a frying pan over a medium heat, add the lardons and fry until crisp. Remove from the pan and drain on kitchen paper.

Melt the 20g of butter in the same pan, add the mushrooms and fry for 2–3 minutes until tender. Remove from the pan and set aside with the bacon.

In the same pan, gently fry the pearl onions for 5–10 minutes until golden and tender, shaking the pan every so often, so that they colour evenly. Add the onions to the bacon and mushrooms.

In a small bowl mix the remaining 2 teaspoons of butter and the plain flour to form a soft paste.

Bring the wine mixture to a gentle simmer and whisk in the butter and flour paste, a little at a time, until the sauce thickens enough to lightly coat the back of a spoon. Add the bacon, mushrooms and pearl onions, and gently reheat the sauce. Season to taste and keep warm.

Bring a pan of heavily salted water to the boil. Break each egg into a ramekin. When the water is boiling, create a whirlpool with the handle of the wooden spoon. Slide one egg into the whirlpool, turn down the heat to simmering and cook for 3–4 minutes until the white is firm but the yolk is still runny. Remove the egg with a slotted spoon and place carefully on a double layer of kitchen paper. Poach the other eggs in the same way.

Meanwhile, heat the remaining 2 tablespoons of oil in a frying pan over a medium heat. Fry the baguette slices until golden brown on both sides. Drain on kitchen paper.

Place a slice of fried baguette on each plate, top with a poached egg and spoon over the sauce. Sprinkle with chopped parsley or chervil for artistic effect and serve immediately.

Oeufs Drumkilbo

They called her Madame Vodka – an accomplished cook, running the kitchen at Drumkilbo a handsome white house in the depths of Perthshire, Scotland. One night, back in the Fifties, some guests arrived late, long after dinner had been cleared away. Lord Elphinstone, whose house it was, asked Madame V to whip up a little midnight snack. So she rootled through larder and icebox and found a few chunks of leftover lobster (this was a grand house, after all), a couple of hard-boiled eggs, a handful of prawns and some diced tomato. With a dash of anchovy essence for depth, and a few jigs of Tabasco, she mixed this with fresh mayonnaise. A delicious melange, but our chef did not stop there. She melted aspic into a soupçon of seafood stock, added it this to the dish, and topped it off with a thin layer of jelly. *Oeufs Drumkilbo* was born – a fairly intricate, if enticing, country house curio, to be wheeled out at various weddings, balls and wakes. But Lord Elphinstone happened to be the Queen Mother's nephew. And after one bite Her Majesty was not only amused, but gave the recipe to her own chef. 'It was one of my grandmother's favourites,' the King told me, after relating this particular tale. And it's still a regular fixture on his menus. A few years back, though, I received an elegant rebuke from one of Lord Elphinstone's descendants, who said that although both the Queen Mother and the King were both fans, and the recipe did come from Drumkilbo, the rest of the story wasn't quite true. Which, come to think of it, makes sense, as leaving aspic to set for an hour hardly amounts to a 'thrown together' meal. Hey ho. It's still a charming tale. This may seem a daunting dish, what with all that fish stock and gelatine. And it's certainly on the richer side of things. But this is one of the recipes that seems more complex than it actually is. And makes for one hell of a smart starter, too.

— Serves 4 —

3 gelatine leaves

500g Scottish lobster meat, cooked

75g peeled cooked prawns

1 hard-boiled egg, diced

3 plum tomatoes, peeled, deseeded and diced

100ml clear fish stock

100g mayonnaise

25ml ketchup

a splash of anchovy essence

a splash of Worcestershire sauce

10g flat-leaf parsley, chopped

a few pinches of chopped chives

salt and freshly ground black pepper

chervil leaves, to garnish

hot brown toast, to serve

Soak the gelatine leaves in a bowl of ice-cold water to soften.

Chop the lobster and prawns into small chunks and place in a large bowl. Add the diced egg and tomatoes.

Warm the fish stock in a small pan until just simmering, then squeeze out the gelatine leaves and stir them into the stock. When dissolved, remove from the heat.

In a separate bowl, mix together the mayonnaise, ketchup, anchovy essence, Worcestershire sauce and a third of the fish stock mixture. Gently fold this sauce into the seafood mixture, then add the herbs and adjust the seasoning.

Spoon into four ramekins or small glass bowls and smooth the tops with a palette knife. Chill in the fridge for 1 hour before topping each with the remaining fish stock mixture, then return to the fridge to set completely.

Serve with hot brown toast on the side.

Trout Meunière

A fresh brown trout is one of the greatest of all fish – sweet, subtle and quietly elegant. But rather difficult to get hold of, unless you're a keen fisherman. Or good friends with a generous one. Prince Phillip had his own small loch at Balmoral, stocked with both brown and rainbow trout. Although it would have been a brave soul who risked being caught dipping their rod without permission. Rainbow trout, once seen as dull and muddy, is a decent alternative. As long as you get them from a farm where the water is clean, clear and fast running. Chalkstream, in Hampshire, is one of my favourites – and is used by the Buckingham Palace kitchens too.

— Serves 2 —

4 tablespoons plain white flour

2 medium trout, gutted

100g butter

juice of 1 lemon

a generous handful of flat-leaf parsley, finely chopped

salt and freshly ground black pepper

1 lemon, halved, to serve

Season the flour with salt and pepper, then roll the fish in the seasoned flour.

Heat half of the butter in a frying pan over a medium heat. When foaming, season and add the fish. Cook for about 4 minutes on each side, or until the skin becomes crisp and golden, and the flesh just about clings to the bone.

Put the fish on a warmed plate, then heat the rest of the butter over a high heat until it starts to turn brown. Do not let it burn. Add the juice of the lemon and the parsley, then pour over the fish.

Serve with lemon halves for squeezing.

Impossible Dishes

'Procure a fine, lively fat turtle,' starts the recipe for turtle soup, a favourite not just of the royal family (Edward VII always had a flask of it to hand), but of aristocrats and plutocrats too. By the start of Elizabeth II's reign, though, it had disappeared from the royal table. With good reason, seeing that around 15,000 turtles (said to taste like a cross between veal and lobster) were shipped live to Britain from the West Indies. Prices were predictably steep, and wild stocks ruinously depleted.

The recipe goes on for pages, including detailed notes on slaughter ('kill the turtle overnight so that it may be left to bleed in a cool place ...') and cutting. The soup also required a leg of beef, knuckle of veal and one old hen. All simmered for six hours, before adding Madeira, herbs and sherry. Even with a large brigade, turtle soup took a serious amount of work.

As did many other dishes. 'When cuisine Classique was taken for granted no one realised the amount of preparation that might go into one dish,' sighed Gabriel Tschumi. *Côtelettes de Bécassines à la Souvaroff*, served at Edward VII's postponed Coronation banquet, involved tiny cutlets of deboned snipe (a small, wading bird), spread with foie gras and game forcemeat, then breadcrumbed, put into a pig's caul, grilled and served with a truffle and Madeira sauce. The King could eat them by the dozen.

Cailles à la Royale was another labour-intensive classic. Deboned quails were simmered in their own stock, the heads removed and reserved, the bodies stuffed with foie gras, then painted with two different glazes, both made from the stock. The heads were reattached using a toothpick, and artificial eyes fashioned from egg white and truffle. Served on a pineapple granita, a good day's worth of work disappeared in a couple of bites.

At Christmas, there was always a boar's head in jelly, stuffed with forcemeat, thin strips of tongue and cheek, bacon, truffles and pistachios. Then carefully sewn up and braised. Alongside, a huge raised pie, in which woodcock went into pheasant, pheasant into chicken, and chicken into turkey. All the birds were boned and surrounded with stuffing, before being entombed in a rich pastry and baked. 'When the pie was sliced,' remembered Tschumi, 'each piece had the different flavours of the birds from which it was made.'

And while there is no actual evidence of Queen Victoria eating roasted cygnet (never swans, being tough, with a nasty fishy tang) at Christmas, her son was an enthusiast. The young bird appears on a Sandringham Christmas menu of the 1890s, as *Cygne à la Windsor*. And in 1908, *The Times* reported that 'at Their Majesties' Christmas dinner one of the special dishes will be roasted cygnets, reared on the Thames, and caught by Mr Abnett, the King's swan master.' Reports of a Boxing Day cygnet curry, though, should be taken with a pinch of salt.

Macaroni au Gratin

One of the very few things Edward VII could not abide was pasta. Tschumi tells the tale of a shooting lunch in November 1903. A well-known Italian diplomat was joining the party and M. Menager, the head chef, suggested that a dish of *Macaroni à l'Italienne* might be included. 'King Edward disliked food as starchy as this and made it quite clear he would have none of it himself, but he consented to macaroni being included on the menu when it was pointed out that the Italian visitor might not care for other dishes.' This version is rather more modern, and contains – I think – a hell of a lot more cheese. I cannot bear those bland, milky, mountebank versions, which are more white sauce than Cheddar. Here, I mix that great Somerset cheese with Gruyère or Comté, for added Alpine heft. Plus some Parmesan on top. I'm sure that exalted Italian gentleman would have approved.

— Serves 6 —

250g smoked streaky bacon or pancetta, cut into small bits	180g Gruyère or Comté cheese, grated
1 teaspoon olive oil	a good jig of Tabasco
40g butter, plus extra for greasing	250g macaroni
40g plain flour	70g Parmesan, finely grated
600ml full-fat milk	30g fresh white breadcrumbs
180g good Cheddar, grated	salt and freshly ground black pepper

Preheat the oven to 200°C/400°F/gas mark 6.

Fry the bacon in the olive oil in a heavy-based pan over a medium heat until crisp. Drain on kitchen paper and set aside.

Melt the butter in a saucepan over a low heat, stir in the flour and cook gently for 3–4 minutes. Add the milk and whisk until smooth, then simmer for 5–10 minutes until thick. Add the Cheddar and Gruyère, and stir until melted, then season with pepper and some Tabasco.

Meanwhile, cook the macaroni in salted boiling water, as per the packet instructions, until al dente. Drain in a colander.

Tip the macaroni into a well-buttered baking dish, add the bacon, then pour over the sauce and mix. Mix the Parmesan with the breadcrumbs and scatter on top. Bake for 35–40 minutes until bubbling, then serve.

Fresh Pappardelle

WITH PORCINI

Wild mushrooms are somewhat of an obsession, with Charles III and Queen Camilla deeply competitive about their hauls. In the late summer, porcinis (also known as penny buns or ceps) are particularly abundant in Scotland, as are the apricot-scented chanterelles, birch bolete and wood hedgehog. The wild harvest is either cooked fresh, preserved in butter or dried for use throughout the year.

— Serves 4 —

400g pappardelle pasta

a big lump of butter

a big glug of olive oil

600g porcini (cep) mushrooms, sliced vertically

1 garlic clove, finely chopped

½ glass of white wine

a handful of chopped flat-leaf parsley

salt and freshly ground black pepper

a big handful of grated Parmesan, to serve

Cook the pasta in plenty of salted water according to the package instructions.

Meanwhile, heat the butter and oil in a large frying pan over a high heat. When hot, add the mushrooms and cook for 5 minutes until all the water has evaporated. Reduce the heat and add the garlic, cooking for a few minutes, then whack the heat back up and deglaze the pan with the wine. Let it evaporate, then add salt and pepper to taste, parsley and a teaspoonful of the pasta cooking water.

Drain the pasta and add to the sauce in the pan, mixing well. Serve with the grated Parmesan.

Asparagus & Spring Vegetable Risotto

This was served at Windsor Castle on Sunday 7 May 2023, just before the Coronation concert. It was the day after the Coronation, and everyone was pretty relieved all had gone so smoothly. It was a beautiful, clear and sultry night, and as dusk fell the castle exploded into light, as thousands of drones and flashing bracelets lit up the gloaming. This recipe uses spring vegetables, but feel free to substitute with mushrooms in autumn, or just have it plain.

— Serves 4 —

50g butter, plus 25g cut into small cubes and kept in the fridge

1 small onion, very finely chopped

300g carnaroli or arborio rice (or vialone nano, although this is more traditionally used for seafood risottos)

200ml dry white wine

1 litre good chicken stock, kept at a rolling boil

25g Parmesan, finely grated, plus extra to serve

12 asparagus spears, steamed for 5 minutes, woody ends removed, then chopped in half

350g peas (frozen or fresh), briefly blanched

sea salt and freshly ground black pepper

Heat the butter in a large, heavy-based saucepan over a low heat. Add the onion and cook to soften for about 10 minutes, stirring from time to time.

Add the rice and cook, stirring, for about 5 minutes until it is white and glistening. Add the wine and cook off the alcohol for a couple of minutes.

Add a ladle of hot stock and cook over a medium-high heat, stirring almost constantly, until the liquid is absorbed. Repeat again and again, only adding more stock when the rice has soaked up the last lot. After 20–25 minutes the rice should be soft yet firm, with a slight grain of crunch in the middle. Every grain should be separately definable in the mouth, yet surge together as one in the pan.

Take off the heat and leave to sit for a minute. Throw in the cold butter cubes and beat the hell out of the risotto with a wooden spoon, shaking the pan until all the butter is incorporated. Add the Parmesan and do the same. Finally, add the peas and asparagus, and mix gently. Season. Serve at once with extra grated Parmesan.

Coronation Food

Even by the sumptuous standards of Edward VII, the Coronation banquet, scheduled for Thursday 26 June 1902, was to be one of history's most lavish dinners. Indeed, the King announced himself 'very pleased indeed' with the menu, created by royal chef Monsieur Menager. The fourteen-course extravaganza would start with *Consommé de Faisan aux Quenelles*, a simple-seeming pheasant soup that took three days of preparation. Not to mention those *Côtelettes de Becassines à la Souvaroff*, minute mouthfuls of foie gras-stuffed snipe, a dish that took the skill of a surgeon, and the patience of Job, to put together. Not forgetting quails in jelly, and Dover sole fillets, gently poached in Chablis, garnished with oysters, mussels and prawns. For pudding, gem-like liqueur jellies, and *Caisses de Fraises Miramare*, involving baskets of spun sugar and jellied strawberries folded into a rich vanilla cream. And so work began, in the kitchens of Buckingham Palace, a full two weeks before the big day.

That June was unseasonably hot, turning the kitchens into a sweaty inferno. And normal cooking service, feeding the hundreds of inhabitants of the palace, both royal and below stairs, had to go on as usual – meaning much of the Coronation work was done late into the night. Tempers were as frayed as a dishwasher's rag. As the kitchen staff cursed and toiled, the ingredients flooded in – 2,500 plump quails, 300 legs of mutton, 80 chickens, dozens of huge sturgeon, chilled boxes of fresh foie gras from Strasbourg and kilos of the finest Russian caviar. Jellies, both for the quail and for the puddings, filled every available container. At last, though, on the eve of the Coronation, and after a fortnight's back-breaking work, everything was ready for the big day.

Then, disaster. Menager was informed by Sir Frederick Treves, the King's surgeon, that the monarch was gravely ill. And the Coronation must be postponed. Edward was suffering from an abscess in his abdomen, and had to be operated on immediately. The first concern of the kitchen was, of course, their King. But once the shock had abated, another worry remained – what the hell were they going to do with all that food?

The jellies were melted down and stored in empty magnums of Champagne, the caviar put on ice and the quails preserved. But the rest – cooked chicken, partridge, sturgeon, cutlets, fruit and cream – was quietly delivered to the Little Sisters of the Poor, to be handed out to the destitute of London's East End. The King recuperated, aboard the *Victoria and Albert*, and the Coronation was rearranged for 9 August. But quite what the denizens of Whitechapel made of some of the most ornately extravagant food ever prepared is lost, very sadly, in the mists of time.

Pulled & Grilled Turkey

This dish is traditionally served at Sandringham on Boxing Day using leftover turkey and is a particular favourite of the King's. Having tried it, I have to agree. Turkey can be the dreariest of birds, and while a Boxing Day curry can make things rather more exciting, this is a post-Christmas cracker that can be enjoyed the whole year around. It's just as good with chicken or pheasant, too.

— Serves 6 —

450g cooked turkey breast

450g cooked brown turkey meat (from the thigh and legs)

mashed potatoes, to serve

For the velouté sauce

35g unsalted butter

35g plain flour

400ml chicken stock

100ml double cream

salt and freshly ground black pepper

For the coating

75g butter, softened

35g plain flour

1 egg yolk

1 tablespoon tomato purée

2 tablespoons mango chutney

1 tablespoon Dijon mustard

a good dash of Tabasco

a good dash of Worcestershire sauce

150g fresh white breadcrumbs

salt and freshly ground black pepper

Slice the turkey breast meat into bite-size pieces and shred the brown meat into pieces of similar size.

To make the velouté sauce for the turkey breast, melt the butter in a medium saucepan over a low-medium heat. Add the flour and cook, stirring constantly, for about 1 minute. Gradually add the chicken stock, whisking continuously, until the sauce thickens and is smooth. Simmer gently for 5 minutes, stirring occasionally to prevent any lumps forming. Season well with salt and pepper, add the cream and remove from the heat.

To make the coating for the brown meat, combine the butter with the flour in a mixing bowl and mix until smooth. Add the egg yolk, tomato purée, mango chutney and Dijon mustard. Add a good dash each of Tabasco and Worcestershire sauce, season with salt and pepper, and mix until smooth and thoroughly combined. Coat the dark turkey meat pieces in the seasoned butter paste, then roll in the breadcrumbs to coat.

Preheat the grill to a medium heat and arrange the breadcrumbed turkey on a lined baking tray. Grill until crisp, golden brown and hot through.

Meanwhile, add the sliced turkey breast to the velouté sauce and place the pan over a medium heat, stirring gently until the sauce and meat are piping hot.

Serve the pulled turkey breast in a warmed bowl alongside the grilled meat, with plenty of mashed potatoes.

Fricassée of Chicken

WITH MORELS & CHERVIL CREAM SAUCE

Another dish served at Windsor Castle before the Coronation concert. It's a classic French recipe, but lightened up for modern tastes. If you can't find morels, use regular mushrooms instead.

— Serves 4 —

200g morel mushrooms

1 large organic, free-range chicken

4 tablespoons light olive oil

3 banana shallots, sliced

2–3 sprigs of thyme

3 sprigs of tarragon

2 bay leaves

250ml dry white wine, such as Chablis

500ml good chicken stock

150ml double cream

25g unsalted butter

16 English asparagus stalks, trimmed of leaves and woody ends

salt and freshly ground black pepper

steamed basmati rice, to serve

Trim the mushrooms and reserve the trimmings. Carefully wash the mushrooms to ensure there is no grit inside the cups. Leave to dry on kitchen paper.

Cut the chicken into 8 or 10 pieces, depending on preference and size of the chicken (thighs, drumsticks, breast into two or three pieces). Cover and chill until ready to cook.

Cut the remaining chicken carcass in half. Heat half the oil in a large saucepan over a high heat, add the carcass pieces and fry until golden brown, turning occasionally to make sure all the little bits of chicken colour but don't burn on the bottom of the pan. Add the sliced shallots, mushroom trimmings, thyme, tarragon and bay leaves, and cook for a minute or so to soften the shallots.

Add the wine to the pan, stir to deglaze, reduce the heat and simmer until the wine has reduced by half. Add the chicken stock, bring to the boil and simmer for about 15 minutes, skimming as you go and allowing the liquid to reduce by about one-third.

Strain the stock into a bowl, discarding the solids, and return it to the wiped-out pan. Add the double cream, season well and bring back to a very gentle simmer.

Season the chicken pieces with salt and pepper. Heat a large frying pan over a medium-high heat, add the remaining oil and gently seal the pieces of chicken in batches, getting a light golden brown on the skin side and just sealing the uncovered flesh side. Add the browned chicken pieces to the sauce, partially cover with a lid and simmer for 15–20 minutes until the breast meat is cooked through, depending on the size of the chicken pieces.

Remove the breast meat from the pan and keep warm, then cook the leg and thigh meat for a further 10 minutes. Return the breast meat to the pan, cover, remove from the heat and allow to rest while you cook the mushrooms and asparagus.

Melt the butter in a frying pan over a medium heat until foaming. Add the mushrooms and sauté until tender.

Meanwhile, blanch the asparagus in salted water for 3–5 minutes until tender.

Garnish the fricassée with the asparagus and sautéed morels, and serve with basmati rice.

Roast Rack of Lamb

The late Queen was known for the simplicity of her tastes, and roast rack of lamb (or *Carré d'Agneau*) is not only simple but a classic, too. It's certainly not the cheapest of cuts (and do try to avoid that rather tasteless spring lamb). The key is to render all that fat in the initial searing, to produce a crisp crust.

— Serves 2 —

1 × 6-bone rack of lamb, French-trimmed	a handful of rosemary and thyme leaves, finely chopped
2 tablespoons olive oil	sea salt and freshly ground black pepper

Preheat the oven to 220°C/425°F/gas mark 7.

Mix 1 tablespoon of the olive oil with the herbs and some salt and pepper. Massage into both sides of the lamb, as well as the ends, and leave for 20 minutes.

Heat the remaining tablespoon of oil in a heavy roasting pan over a high heat and brown the rack all over, fat-side first, for about 3 minutes, then on the bottom for about 2 minutes. Place in the oven, fat-side up, for 15 minutes.

Rest for 5 minutes before serving.

*Roast Rack of Lamb, Petits
Pois à la Française and
Pommes Elizabeth
(clockwise from left)*

Petits Pois à la Française

You'll find this dish on the early summer menus of all the monarchs, using a mixture of fresh new peas and lettuce. Now, of course, the frozen pea is ubiquitous (and very fine too), and lettuce is available all year round. It can be served on its own (eaten with a couple of slices of thick toast) or as a vegetable side dish. Without the help of a vast kitchen staff, podding peas can become rather a bore. I'd far rather eat them raw, with a small pile of salt. Use frozen for the recipe below.

— Serves 4 —

75g butter

500g frozen peas, defrosted and drained (or 1kg fresh peas, shelled)

12 small shallots, peeled and sliced

1 cos or romaine lettuce, shredded, but not too finely

a handful of mint, parsley and/or chervil, washed and roughly torn

50ml white wine

a splash of chicken stock or water

a big pinch of salt

Melt half of the butter in a large saucepan, then add the peas, shallots, lettuce, herbs, white wine and stock. Bring to a simmer, then add the rest of the butter, cover and cook very gently for about 25 minutes, giving the pan an occasional shake.

Check the seasoning and serve.

Pictured on previous page

Pommes Elizabeth

Pommes Elizabeth is a classical dish from the royal repertoire, which Mark Flanagan's Buckingham Palace chefs 'adapted to suit the late Queen'. It's a simple potato croquette with cooked spinach in the middle, shaped into a 'pear' so 'they stand up proudly in the dish when presented'. It was served (as it also was at many other dinners both formal and private) alongside the lamb at the state banquet held in honour of President Trump.

— Makes 8 croquettes —

800g floury potatoes, cut into chunks

40g butter

2 egg yolks

600g spinach, washed

a big glug of olive oil, for frying

sea salt and freshly ground black pepper

For coating

50g plain flour

2 whole eggs, beaten

120g breadcrumbs

Bring a big pan of water to the boil, add the potatoes and a good whack of salt, and simmer for 15–20 minutes until soft. Drain, then put through a potato ricer into a bowl. Beat in the butter and egg yolks, season, cover and leave to cool.

Bring a saucepan half-filled with water to the boil, or use a steamer. Add the spinach and cook for about 1 minute, then drain, allow to cool and squeeze out the excess water. Place in a bowl, add 2 big pinches of sea salt and mix in.

Shape the potato mixture into eight pear shapes, each the size of a baby's fist, pressing a ball of cooked spinach into the centre of each one.

Put the flour, eggs and breadcrumbs for coating into three separate, shallow dishes. Dip each croquette in flour first, then into the egg, then the breadcrumbs. Place on a tray and chill in the fridge for 30 minutes.

Heat the olive oil in a large frying pan and cook the croquettes in batches of four, turning regularly until crisp and golden all over. Drain on kitchen paper and serve hot.

Pictured on previous page

Beef Wellington

The Duke of Wellington, conqueror of Napoleon and inspiration for the rubber boot, was one of Queen Victoria's favourites, 'our immortal hero,' in her words, both mentor and confidante. An enthusiastic gossip, as he grew older and steadily more deaf, he tended to shout rather than whisper tales of various indiscretions, meaning the entire table (usually including the subject of his scurrilous chat) could hear every word. A sharp look from the Queen, though, was all that was needed to shut him up. Famously uninterested in food, one story goes that Beef Wellington was the only dish he would eat. Another claims it was simply a patriotic rebranding, during the Napoleonic Wars, of the French *Filet de Bouef en Croûte*. Whatever the truth, it's a classic of the royal table. This recipe comes from Jamie Shears, Executive Chef of the Mount St. Restaurant. It opened in 2022 and two of the first guests were the King and Queen. You could also substitute a fillet of venison for the beef.

— Serves 4 —

750g good-quality, centre-cut, dry-aged beef fillet, trimmed of excess fat and sinew

1–2 tablespoons olive oil

60g unsalted butter

1–2 tablespoons English mustard

2 banana shallots

250g chestnut mushrooms, trimmed

leaves from 2 sprigs of thyme

1 skinless, boneless chicken breast

100ml double cream

3 eggs

60ml full-fat milk

60g plain flour, plus extra for dusting

2 tablespoons finely chopped parsley

500g puff pastry

salt and freshly ground black pepper

Season the beef generously with salt and pepper. Heat 1 tablespoon of the oil and 25g of the butter in a large frying pan over a high heat. When the butter is foaming and the pan is hot, add the beef and sear on all sides to a deep golden-brown colour. Remove from the pan and leave to cool. Do not wash the pan as you need it again. Leave the beef to cool and then brush with the English mustard to coat.

Finely dice the shallots and tip into the frying pan with another 25g of the butter and sweat over a low heat for about 5 minutes until soft.

Roughly chop the mushrooms, then tip into a food processor and pulse until finely chopped. Add the mushrooms and thyme leaves to the frying pan, season, increase the heat to medium and cook for about 10 minutes, stirring often until all the moisture has evaporated. Tip the mixture into a bowl and leave to cool.

continued overleaf

Dice the chicken breast, then blitz in a food processor until smooth. Add the double cream, season and mix again to combine. Add this paste to the cold mushrooms, mix until smooth, then cover and chill until ready to use.

Make a crêpe batter by whisking two of the eggs with the milk and flour until smooth. Add the chopped parsley and season. Beat the remaining egg in a separate small bowl and set aside.

Melt the remaining 10g of butter in a non-stick 20cm frying pan over a medium heat. Pour in a thin layer of the batter to make a pancake and cook for about 1 minute until golden on the underside. Flip the pancake over and cook for a further 30 seconds. Remove from the pan and repeat to make 3–4 pancakes in total. Leave to cool.

Lightly dust the work surface with flour and roll out the puff pastry to a 30 × 40cm rectangle. Arrange the crêpes, slightly overlapping, down the length of the pastry, leaving a 2cm border all around. Spread the pancakes with the mushroom mixture and place the seared mustard-coated beef fillet on top. Brush the edges of the pastry with the beaten egg and fold the sides in, brush with egg again, then roll the pastry around the beef in a tight cylinder. Cover tightly with clingfilm and chill in the fridge for at least 1 hour or up to 4 hours to set.

When ready to cook, preheat the oven to 200°C/400°F/gas mark 6.

Unwrap the Wellington from the clingfilm and place on a lined baking tray. Brush the pastry with beaten egg to glaze and cook for 45–50 minutes until the pastry is crisp and golden brown. After 45 minutes the beef will be medium rare; after 50 minutes it will be medium.

Remove from the oven and rest for 20 minutes. Slice your Wellington into four thick slices to serve.

Trilogy of Mutton

'The recipe for the Trilogy of Mutton was specially created for the Prince of Wales and the launch of the Mutton Renaissance Campaign,' says John Williams, Executive Chef at The Ritz, and a man who has cooked for the Queen Mother, Queen Elizabeth II, and the King. 'His Majesty wanted to show the versatility of mutton, having it served as a trilogy. I felt very honoured as the occasion was to popularise mutton, which had gone out of fashion. Ultimately, it was to help the farmers who were losing money on mutton, only receiving very small amounts of money for the fleece. We had to help the farmers get a fair price. The lunch was held in the Ritz Restaurant and there were lots of dignitaries, but without the Prince of Wales, now King Charles III, this would simply not have taken off. But, rest assured, it certainly did with the King behind it!'

Slow Pot Roast Loin

OF HERDWICK MUTTON

Ask the butcher for the mutton bones from prepping the loin, which should be added to the cooking liquor to give extra flavour to the sauce. Serve with roast mixed vegetables, such as carrots, parsnips and beetroot, and creamed potatoes finished with Gruyère cheese and chives.

— Serves 6 —

2 tablespoons light olive oil

1kg boned and rolled mutton loin (ideally Herdwick; ask the butcher for the bones)

1 small onion, diced

1 small carrot, diced

1 small leek, diced

½ celery stick, diced

5 garlic cloves, peeled

1 bouquet garni (1 sprig each of

thyme, parsley and tarragon and 1 bay leaf)

200ml white wine

500ml rich brown veal or chicken stock

50g unsalted butter, at room temperature, diced

1 sprig each of tarragon, parsley and mint, leaves finely chopped

salt and freshly ground black pepper

Preheat the oven to 150°C/300°F/gas mark 2.

Heat the oil in a heavy ovenproof casserole dish over a high heat. Season the mutton, add to the pot and brown well on all sides. Remove the mutton from the pot and set aside.

Continued overleaf and pictured on page 180

Add the mutton bones to the pot, if using, and brown these too.

Add the onion, carrot, leek, celery and whole garlic cloves to the pot, reduce the heat to low and gently sweat the vegetables for about 10 minutes, stirring often, until softened. Add the bouquet garni, pour in the wine and reduce by half. Add the stock, bring back to the boil and place the mutton on top of the vegetables (and bones, if using) so the meat is half submerged in the cooking liquor.

Cover with foil or a lid, place in the oven and slowly braise for about 2 hours until the mutton is tender. Remove the foil or lid, baste the meat with the braising liquor and continue to cook for a further 20 minutes until it is beautifully glazed.

Once the meat is tender and glazed, remove from the braising liquor, cover and keep warm. Pass the braising liquor through a fine sieve into a clean pan, making sure that the garlic cloves are pushed through the sieve to act as a liaison and flavouring for the sauce. Leave the sauce to settle for 10 minutes to allow the fat to rise to the top. Spoon off the fat, place the pan over a low heat and bring to a simmer. Whisk in the butter to make the sauce glossy and rich. Season to taste and finish with finely chopped tarragon, parsley and mint.

Serve the mutton sliced with the sauce poured over.

Mutton Pies

You *can* use lamb here instead, neck or leg, although mutton has rather more flavour.

— Makes 10 pies —

600g boneless mutton leg

2 tablespoons olive oil

1 banana shallot, peeled

1 small carrot, peeled and trimmed

½ celery stick

1 garlic clove, crushed

2 teaspoons tomato purée

250ml veal or beef stock

1 fresh bay leaf

1 sprig of thyme

1 sprig of rosemary

100ml Madeira

600g puff pastry

plain flour, for dusting

1 egg, beaten

salt and freshly ground black pepper

You will need

10cm plain cutter

11cm plain cutter

Cut the mutton into large dice. Heat the oil in a frying pan over a high heat and brown the mutton in batches until nicely caramelised. Remove from the pan and place in a lidded casserole dish.

Finely chop the shallot, carrot and celery, add to the frying pan and cook over a low heat for about 10 minutes until softened. Add the garlic and tomato purée, and cook for a further minute. Deglaze the pan with the stock, season, bring to the boil and pour into the casserole along with the herbs.

Cover and simmer very gently for 2–3 hours, stirring from time to time, until the mutton is completely tender and starting to fall apart. (Alternatively, you can cook the mutton in an oven heated to 150°C/300°F/gas mark 2 for 3 hours, or until tender – or use a pressure cooker, if you have one).

Remove the herbs, add the Madeira and continue to cook over a low heat, stirring to break down the strands of meat and to reduce the Madeira to almost nothing.

Season to taste and allow to cool.

Roll out the puff pastry on a lightly floured work surface to a thickness of 2mm and use the cutters to stamp out ten 10cm discs and ten 11cm discs. Arrange the smaller pastry discs on a lined baking sheet. Spoon a good tablespoon of the cold mutton into the middle of these pastry discs, leaving a 1cm border. Brush the border with beaten egg and cover with the larger pastry discs, pressing the edges together to seal. Brush the tops of the pies with beaten egg, decoratively mark the tops with a cocktail stick or the point of a sharp knife and score a hole in the top of each pie. Chill the pies for 1 hour, or until ready to bake.

Preheat the oven to 180°C/350°F/gas mark 4.

Bake the pies for about 25 minutes until golden brown and crisp.

Pictured overleaf

*Slow Pot Roast Loin of
Herdwick Mutton,
Mutton Pies and Welsh
Mountain Mutton Stew
(clockwise from left)*

Welsh Mountain Mutton Stew

Mutton has the most dull and dowdy of reputations, seen as tough, tallowy and the sort of beast enjoyed only by rotund Dickensian types with scarlet noses and a serious case of gout. Which is a crying shame, as it can be the most majestic of meats, having lived long enough to know a thing or two about flavour. OK, so the very old brutes can be a little overpowering. But give me a hogget, which is a lamb over one year old, over that dreary, tasteless spring lamb any day. The King is right – mutton really is a magnificent meat and this stew shows exactly why.

— Serves 4 —

600g middle neck of mutton

a good pinch of caster sugar

1 tablespoon light olive oil

25g butter

½ onion, diced

1 small carrot, diced

½ leek, diced

½ fennel bulb, diced

1 small celery stick, diced

1 garlic clove, crushed

1 tablespoon tomato purée

1 tablespoon plain flour

500ml brown chicken or veal stock

3 tomatoes, peeled, deseeded and diced

1 faggot of herbs (a tied bunch of 2 sprigs each of parsley and thyme and 1 bay leaf)

salt and freshly ground black pepper

To garnish

12 small new potatoes

12 baby turnips

12 baby carrots

12 button onions

20g podded broad beans

25g butter

a pinch of caster sugar

1 tablespoon chopped chives

1 tablespoon chopped flat-leaf parsley

salt and freshly ground black pepper

Preheat the oven to 150°C/300°F/gas mark 2.

Cut the mutton into equal-size pieces, each about 25g, and season well with salt, pepper and a pinch of sugar. Heat the oil and butter in a heavy ovenproof casserole dish over a high heat, then brown the mutton in batches until nicely caramelised. The sugar settles slowly on the bottom of the pan where it turns to caramel and will ultimately give the required colour to the sauce.

Remove the meat from the pan and drain off some of the fat. Add the diced onion, carrot, leek, fennel and celery to the pot along with the crushed garlic. Sweat over a low-medium heat for a few minutes until the vegetables have softened. Add the tomato purée and flour, stir to combine and cook for a few minutes more until caramelised.

Slowly add the stock, stirring continuously until smooth. Add the diced tomatoes, return the meat to the pot, add the faggot of herbs and bring to the boil. Use a slotted spoon to remove any scum that forms on the top. Cover with a lid and braise in the oven for about 2 hours until the meat is tender.

Meanwhile, wash and trim the vegetables for the garnish. Heat the butter in a sauté pan, add the potatoes and turnips along with 100ml water and cook over a medium heat for about 10 minutes until the vegetables are just tender. Add the carrots and onions and cook for 5 minutes more. Add the broad beans, season with salt, pepper and a pinch of sugar, and cook for another minute until the vegetables are nicely glazed.

Remove the meat from the casserole and strain the braising liquor into a bowl. Return the meat and sauce to the casserole, add the glazed vegetables and season to taste. Scatter with chopped chives and parsley to serve.

Roast Saddle of Lamb

WITH HERB STUFFING & PORT SAUCE

This was a dish served at the state banquet held in honour of Donald Trump, a man not exactly known for his gilded palate. Still, Mark Flanagan composed a typically elegant menu: steamed halibut with a watercress mousse and chervil sauce, for the starter; pudding was a strawberry sablé with lemon verbena ice cream; while the main course was herb-stuffed saddle of lamb, with a port sauce.

— Serves 4 —

1 saddle of lamb, boned, rolled and tied by the butcher

a big glug of olive oil

salt and freshly ground black pepper

For the stuffing

2 onions, finely chopped

4 garlic cloves, finely chopped

2 tablespoons chopped thyme

2 tablespoons chopped rosemary

1 tablespoon chopped parsley

zest and juice of 1 lemon

2 anchovies, finely chopped

150g breadcrumbs

1 egg

salt and freshly ground black pepper

For the port sauce

50g butter

2 shallots, finely chopped

2 garlic cloves, finely chopped

1 carrot, diced

1 celery stick, finely chopped

1 teaspoon finely chopped rosemary

1 teaspoon finely chopped thyme

250ml decent port

350ml beef stock

a lusty shake of Worcestershire sauce

salt and freshly ground black pepper

Preheat the oven to 220°C/425°F/gas mark 7.

Mix all the stuffing ingredients in a bowl.

Open up the saddle of lamb, fill with the stuffing mixture, then roll up tightly, using three pieces of string to secure. Rub with the olive oil, season well and roast in the oven for 20 minutes, before turning it down to 180°C/350°F/gas mark 4 to cook for another hour.

Remove and allow to rest for 15 minutes while you make the sauce.

Melt the butter in a frying pan over a medium heat. Once foaming, add the shallots and garlic, and cook until soft but not browned, about 10 minutes. Add the vegetables and herbs, and cook for another 6–8 minutes.

Turn up the heat, add the port and burn off all the booze. When you can no longer smell alcohol, it's ready. Add any juices from the resting lamb, then add the stock and Worcestershire sauce, and cook until reduced by half. Season, then strain through a sieve into a gravy boat. Serve alongside the lamb.

Savouries

A course popular in Victorian and Edwardian times, savouries would appear between the main course and pudding. Invariably strong flavoured (through salt and spice), and often appearing on toast, they made, according to food writer Ambrose Heath (who devoted a whole tome, *Good Savouries*, to this delectable subject), 'an admirable ending to a meal, like some unexpected witticism or amusing epigram at the close of a pleasant conversation. It has the last word, as it were, before we turn to the frivolities of dessert.'

Edward VII far preferred savouries to sweet pudding, and you'll find various versions scattered through the royal menus, right up until Elizabeth II. According to Charles Oliver, 'when the Prince [Phillip] is away, and the Queen dines alone at Buckingham Palace, often she will settle for just a savoury – perhaps some flaked haddock in scrambled egg, served with a thin piece of toast.'

The following six savouries all make good suppers too, if an eight-course banquet seems too much of a stretch.

Scotch Woodcock

A classic savoury, found in palaces and gentlemen's clubs alike. The Queen Mother was a particular fan.

— Serves 4 as a savoury —

4 eggs

a big lump of butter, plus extra to serve (optional)

2 slices of bread, crusts removed

a smidgin of Gentleman's Relish, to serve (optional)

8 tinned or bottled anchovies

salt and freshly ground black pepper

Beat the eggs briefly, and season with salt and pepper.

Melt the butter over low heat, until foaming. Add the eggs and cook very slowly, stirring constantly. After about 10 minutes, they should still be a mixture of set and runny.

In the meantime, toast the bread, then spread with the extra butter or a thin layer of Gentleman's Relish.

Cut the toast into triangles and top each triangle with scrambled egg and 2 anchovies to serve.

Croque Monsieur

This is not the croque monsieur as we know it, as it omits béchamel sauce. Cut into rounds with a 2-inch circular pastry cutter, or simply use whole slices of bread.

— Serves 4 as a savoury —

4 slices of thin white bread, buttered on the outside

150g Gruyère cheese, thinly sliced

2 slices of good ham

50g butter, for cooking

freshly ground black pepper

Either: Cut the bread, cheese and ham into the same-sized shapes. Layer a slice of bread on the bottom (with buttered-side down), then add a slice of cheese, then ham, then cheese. Season with pepper and place another slice of bread on top, buttered-side upwards. Press down gently. Or, just layer in the same order, but using whole slices of bread, cheese and ham.

Melt the butter in a frying pan over a medium heat . Cook the sandwiches for about 2 minutes on each side until crisp, golden and oozing cheese.

Beignets au Fromage

Hot, savoury, cheesy doughnuts.

— Serves 6 as a savoury —

280ml milk

115g unsalted butter

a big pinch of salt

230g plain white flour

6 eggs

155g Gruyère cheese, grated

500ml vegetable oil, for frying

Put the butter, milk and salt into a saucepan and bring to the boil. Remove from the heat and stir in the flour, then return to a medium heat and stir until you have a thickish batter.

Remove the pan from the heat and whisk in the eggs, one by one. Add 125g of the Gruyère and stir.

Heat the oil in a large, deep pan until shimmering. Add a dessertspoon of batter for each beignet and fry, about three at a time, until golden brown. Drain on kitchen paper and serve scattered with more Gruyère cheese.

Pictured overleaf

*Croque Monsieur,
Scotch Woodcock and
Beignets au Fromage
(clockwise from top left)*

Canapés Ivanhoe

Another savoury classic, and a favourite of Edward VII. Some versions (including the one adored by Elizabeth II) also add scrambled egg. In which case, make the scrambled eggs as on page 147, then add to the haddock and cream mixture and serve atop fried bread.

— Serves 4 as a savoury —

200ml milk

2 smoked haddock fillets

20g butter

50ml double cream

a twist of black pepper

a big pinch of cayenne pepper

2 slices of white bread, crusts removed, fried in butter until crisp and golden and cut into rounds, to serve

Put the milk into a pan and heat gently, add the haddock, then simmer very gently for about 5 minutes until heated through. Remove the fish with a slotted spoon to drain on kitchen paper, then break into large flakes.

Heat the butter in a separate pan, add the flaked haddock and cook for a minute, then add the cream, black pepper and cayenne pepper. Cook for a couple of minutes more, then pile the haddock onto the fried bread rounds to serve.

Sardine Cigarettes

A good cocktail snack, as well as a crisp savoury, these have both salt and a sly chilli heat.

— Makes 10–12 —

2 × 140g tins of good-quality sardines in oil

a good squeeze of fresh lemon juice

a few shakes of Tabasco

a pinch of cayenne pepper

4 sheets of filo pastry

2 tablespoons melted butter

500ml vegetable oil, for frying

salt and freshly ground black pepper

Drain the sardines and remove the backbones. Tip into a bowl and mash the fish with a fork. Add the lemon juice and Tabasco, and season with a good pinch of cayenne, salt and freshly ground black pepper.

Cut the filo pastry into strips 10cm wide and 15–20cm long. Spoon the sardine mixture neatly at the top of each strip, leaving a little gap at the edges. Lightly brush the pastry

with melted butter, fold in the sides to encase the sardine paste and then roll into a cigarette shape.

Heat the vegetable oil in a deep frying pan or wok over a medium heat until a piece of white bread fizzes, browns quickly and floats to the surface. Fry the sardine cigarettes in batches of three or four for 1–2 minutes until golden brown and crisp. Drain on kitchen paper and serve while still very hot.

Smoked Haddock Soufflé

This soufflé was also classed as a savoury. Not just at the end of dinner, but as a light supper for the late Queen, and King Charles III too. Don't be daunted. It may seem a work of culinary alchemy but it's really very easy to get right. The only proviso is to make sure everyone is ready to eat when it emerges from the oven. A soufflé waits for no one. During my research, though, I stumbled across a story (courtesy of The Greasy Spoon blog) involving that slightly bonkers TV cook, Fanny Cradock, and the Duke of Windsor. Apparently, they dined together in his Paris house in 1956, and she took away his recipe for haddock soufflé. Stranger things, as they say, have happened at sea.

— Serves 4 as a starter —

250g undyed smoked haddock

300ml full-fat milk

150ml single cream

50g unsalted butter, plus extra for greasing

50g plain flour

100g Parmesan, freshly grated

1 teaspoon dry English mustard powder

2 egg yolks plus 8 egg whites

salt and freshly ground black pepper

You will need

20cm soufflé dish or ovenproof dish with a capacity of 2 litres, greased with butter

Gently poach the haddock in the milk and cream at a gentle simmer over a low-medium heat for about 10 minutes. Remove the fish from the pan, cool slightly and flake, removing any skin and bones. Reserve the milk mixture.

Preheat the oven to 200°C/400°F/gas mark 6.

Melt the butter in a saucepan over a medium heat. Add the flour, mix well and cook for a minute, stirring continuously. Add a quarter of the reserved milk and cream mixture, and keep stirring over a medium heat until smooth. Add the next quarter of milk along with half of the cheese and beat until smooth.

Add the remaining milk and cheese along with the mustard powder and season well with salt and pepper. Mix until the sauce is smooth, then remove from the heat and beat for about 1 minute to release some of the steam and to cool the sauce slightly.

Scoop the sauce into a large mixing bowl, add the flaked haddock and egg yolks, and mix to combine.

In another clean, large bowl whisk the egg whites to stiff peaks. Using a large metal spoon (preferably silver but never wooden) fold a good spoonful of the egg whites into the sauce

to lighten the mixture and then fold in the remainder, being careful not to knock out too much air.

Spoon the mixture into the buttered dish and spread level. Place the dish on a baking tray and bake the soufflé in the bottom third of the oven for about 40 minutes until well risen, golden brown and with a slight wobble in the middle.

Serve *tout de suite*.

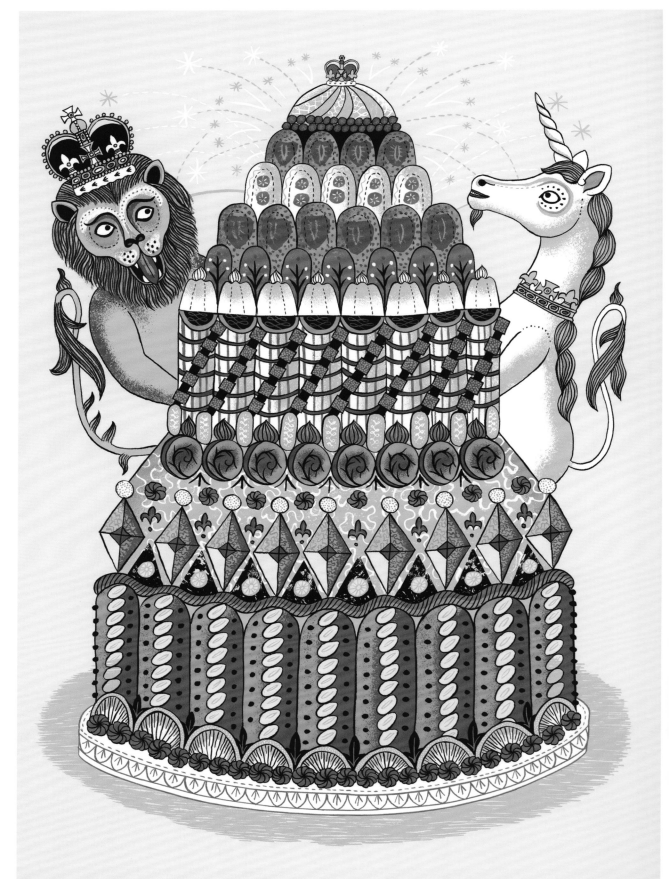

Puddings

Puddings

At their towering, technicolored peak, royal desserts were not so much sweet delights as pure edible architecture, Baroque masterpieces that seduced the eye and wooed the palate. In the days of service *à la française*, they would be part of the *entremets* course, served alongside vegetables and other savoury dishes, as well as choux buns, *savarin au kirsch*, pineapple cakes, fruit tarts, jellies and creams, nougats, meringues and spun-sugar baskets.

Ice cream was churned by hand and made in dozens of different flavours, from vanilla and chocolate through to cucumber, quince, rose water and bergamot. It was often shaped into elaborate bombes, made in special round moulds, while sorbets, spiked with brandy, rum and Grand Marnier, were served as palate cleansers between courses. Ice was taken from the ponds and lakes of royal estates, stored in specially built ice houses at Windsor and Osborne, and delivered to London when needed. 'Home ice', as it was called, was seen as markedly superior to the industrially frozen stuff bought in London. It lasted longer, and was easier to work with.

A quick glance through the cookbook of Charles Elmé Francatelli, who was chief cook to Queen Victoria from 1840 to 1842, shows the most ornate and incredible desserts, towering works of the confectioner's art: *Croquant of Oranges*, where paper-thin slices of orange flesh were dipped in sugar syrup, and then painstakingly attached to a cylindrical croquant mould. Which was stuffed with strawberries and whipped cream flavoured with maraschino. Or his *Pommes à la Portugaise*, a *pâté-chaud* case filled with baked apples, apple marmalade and pastry custard, before being topped with meringue. The whole dish, which resembles the bejewelled turban of some fabulously wealthy grand vizier, is decorated with strips of redcurrant and apple jellies, 'which will produce a very pretty effect.' Flowers were painted, in coloured sugar, all around the base. 'None of these were the simple domestic versions of the Mrs Beetons and Eliza Actons of the Victorian world,' notes Annie Gray. 'Instead, they were moulded, piped, garnished, spiced, shaped, sieved and pounded until the results bore little hint of the raw ingredients, and were elevated into edible art.'

Royal kitchens had copper moulds in every conceivable shape and size, from tiny darioles for making sweetmeats and biscuits to great towering tubs for jellies and blancmange. The pastry section at both Windsor and Buckingham Place was separate from the main kitchen, cooler and rather less frantic. There were waffle irons, pancake pans and iron sheets for pastry. Everything was made from scratch, including the gelatine, laboriously extracted from calves' feet, taking days to render and clarify. The amount of sugar used was astonishing. In 1844, the kitchen got through over 2,000lb of sugar (bought in 14lb sugar loaves), single, double and triple refined, as well as candy and Lisbon sugar, which was very fine and had a particularly fine flavour. All that in just one month.

'The Palace bakers, confectioners and pastry cooks ... were craftsmen,' remembered Gabriel Tschumi, 'and some of the finest work I have ever seen was on the sugar baskets for a dessert called Miramare.' This dish took three days to prepare, and was served at the Coronation of Edward VII. Baskets, measuring six by four inches, were made from sugar paste. 'The handle and lid of each basket was in perfect proportion, to the base, and the sugar paste was coloured to give a grained effect like dark oak.' They were filled with vanilla cream and strawberry jelly, with fresh strawberries added at the end.

Queen Victoria was renowned for her sweet tooth, as was Queen Alexandra (unlike her husband, who preferred savouries) and the latter's favourite pudding was her native Danish berry dish, Rødgrød. Her birthday cakes were legendary, too: five tiers of rich fruit cake, made using forty eggs and lashings of rum and brandy. At Christmas, 300lb of pudding mixture was made, containing four gallons of strong ale, a bottle of rum and a bottle of brandy. All stirred by hand, it was divided into 150 two-pound puddings, given out to all of the staff.

Queen Mary was also known for her love of all things sweet (her husband favoured apple charlotte, plum pudding and pancakes), and always had a huge box of chocolates open on a table in her sitting room. And while the rationing of the two world wars saw sugar in very short supply indeed, puddings continued to play an essential role in any royal meal, private or state, where the Queen Mother and Elizabeth II would mix hearty English classics (Eton mess, treacle tart, fools, bread-and-butter pudding) with French favourites too (soufflés, Peach Melba, crème brûlée and fruit compotes). The very essence, in short, of all royal eating.

Fraises à la Chantilly

Strawberries are the very quintessence of British summer, and have long been grown in the kitchen gardens of Windsor, Sandringham and Balmoral. They were (and still are) regular fixtures on all royal menus in the summer, ranging from garden parties to Ascot lunches, afternoon teas and Derby dinners alike.

— Serves 4 —

8 sponge fingers

750g strawberries

caster sugar, to taste

500ml double cream

Line the bottom of four individual glass dessert bowls with two sponge fingers, cut to fit. Divide 500g of the whole strawberries among the bowls.

Blitz the remaining 250g strawberries with a few pinches of caster sugar to a purée in a food processor, adjusting the sweetness to taste. Pour the purée over the strawberries.

Whip the cream to soft peaks and spoon on top to serve.

Eton Mess

This classic English pudding is said to have been invented at the eponymous school, and served on its speech day on 4 June. Although in the five years I spent there, I never saw any evidence of it. Or tasted so much as a morsel.

— Serves 4 —

2 egg whites
a pinch of salt
125g caster sugar

500g strawberries, hulled and halved
1 tablespoon icing sugar
500ml double cream

Preheat the oven to 130°C/250°F/gas mark ½ and line a baking sheet with baking paper.

Whisk the egg whites with a pinch of salt until they form soft peaks. Gradually add the caster sugar, spoonful by spoonful, whisking continuously until thoroughly combined and the meringue is smooth, glossy and holds stiff peaks.

Spoon the meringue into eight mounds onto the lined baking sheet and cook for 1 hour. Turn off the oven and leave the meringues inside for at least 2 hours, until cold.

Throw half of the strawberries into a blender with the icing sugar and blitz to a purée. Pass the purée through a fine sieve to remove any seeds and set aside.

In a large bowl, whip the cream until not quite firm. Roughly chop the remaining strawberries and add to the cream with the meringues broken into evenly sized shards. Carefully fold everything together. Add most of the strawberry purée and fold again until rippled through the cream mixture.

Spoon into bowls, drizzle with the remaining purée and serve at once.

Lemon Meringue Tartlets

We had these at the lunch following the King's Coronation, in May 2023. The key is the contrast between tart curd and sweet, billowing meringue topping.

— Makes 4 —

For the curd

zest and juice of 3 unwaxed lemons

60g unsalted butter

80g caster sugar

2 eggs, beaten

You will need

4 × 10cm tart tins

baking beans

For the tarts

250g shortcrust pastry (homemade is best, but good shop-bought will do – but ONLY made with butter)

2 egg whites

25g sugar

a dribble of white wine vinegar

First, make curd. Put the lemon zest and juice, butter and sugar into a heatproof bowl set over a pan of simmering water. Stir until all melted and mixed together, then use a whisk to stir in the beaten eggs. Whisk gently for about 10 minutes until it has a thick, curd-like consistency. Pour through a sieve into a bowl. (You can store any left over in the fridge in a sterilised jar.)

Preheat the oven to 180°C/350°F/gas mark 4.

Roll the pastry out thinly and use it to line the tart tins, leaving a little extra pastry overhanging the edges. Place the tins on a lined baking tray. Prick the bases with a fork, line each case with foil, fill with baking beans and blind bake for 20 minutes (removing the beans after 15 minutes) until the pastry is a gentle brown.

Allow to cool, then level off the top of the pastry cases with a knife. Spoon the curd into the cases.

Whisk the egg whites with the sugar into stiff peaks. Dollop generously on top of the curd, then bake for a further 15 minutes until the meringue is browned.

Bananes au Caramel

Alma McKee was cook to both Queen Elizabeth II and the Queen Mother. And this recipe came about one day when she was cooking lunch for the latter at Clarence House. The meat course had gone up, when she suddenly realised there was no pudding. 'I can remember there was a certain amount of panic about what to do next.' Save, that is, for a few bananas.

— Serves 4 —

4 bananas

2 tablespoons caster sugar

50g unsalted butter, plus extra for greasing

100ml double cream

2 tablespoons golden syrup

Peel the bananas and cut through the middle, then cut in half again. Tip into a bowl, add the sugar and mix to combine.

Melt the butter in a frying pan over a medium heat. When the butter is foaming, add the sugared banana pieces and fry gently until they caramelise.

Tip the bananas into a bowl and cool slightly. Roughly chop the bananas, add the cream, mix well to thicken and divide between four individual sundae glasses. Chill while you make the caramel.

Grease a metal baking tray with butter. Pour the syrup into a frying pan and cook over a medium heat, stirring often with a spatula until the syrup turns a deep amber colour. Pour over the greased tray and leave to cool and harden. Break the hardened syrup into small shards, sprinkle over the banana cream and serve immediately.

Coupes Montreuil

OR COUPES MALMAISON

A favourite of Queen Mary's, this is little more than vanilla ice cream with peaches. You can make your own, or just buy some good-quality shop stuff. To make Coupes Malmaison, substitute the peaches with peeled white grapes, topped with a little champagne.

— Serves 4 —

4 ripe peaches, pitted and sliced

a few drops of lemon juice

450ml good vanilla ice cream

Layer the peach slices in dessert glasses, allowing half per person. Sprinkle with a little lemon juice to stop them turning brown.

Top each serving with 2 large scoops of vanilla ice cream.

Cherry Tart

This is a classic summer tart, and adapted from one of Mildred Dorothy Nicholl's recipes (see page 124). Try to buy your cherries direct from the farmer, rather than using those buxom but boring supermarket specimens.

— Serves 6–8 —

For the pastry

200g plain flour, plus extra for rolling out

a pinch of salt

100g unsalted butter, chilled and diced

2 tablespoons caster sugar

1 egg yolk

2 tablespoons ice-cold water, or as needed

1 teaspoon lemon juice

For the frangipane

125g unsalted butter, at room temperature

125g caster sugar

1 teaspoon vanilla bean paste

2 eggs, lightly beaten

finely grated zest of ½ lemon

125g ground almonds

1 tablespoon plain flour

a pinch of salt

To finish

2 tablespoons cherry jam

400g Morello cherries, pitted

30g flaked almonds

icing sugar, for dusting

You will need

20cm tart tin with removable base and depth of 4cm

baking beans

To make the pastry, tip the flour and a pinch of salt into a bowl, then add the cold diced butter. Using your fingers, rub the butter into the flour until the mixture is the texture is of fine sand with only very small flecks of butter remaining. Add the sugar and mix to combine. Add the egg yolk, cold water and lemon juice, and mix to combine using a round-bladed knife, adding more water if needed to bring the mixture together. Knead lightly to gather the dough into a ball, flatten into a disc, cover and chill for 1 hour.

Lightly dust the work surface with flour, roll out the pastry and use to line the tart tin. Prick the bottom all over with a fork and chill again for 20 minutes while you preheat the oven to 190°C/375°F/gas mark 5.

Line the pastry case with foil, fill with baking beans and blind bake for 20 minutes. Remove the foil and beans, and bake for a further 2 minutes to dry out the base. Turn the oven down to 170°C/325°F/gas mark 3.

To make the frangipane, cream together the softened butter, caster sugar and vanilla bean paste until pale and light. This is easiest in a stand mixer or using electric hand-held beaters. Add the eggs, one at a time, mixing well between each addition. Add the grated lemon zest and mix again before adding the ground almonds, flour and salt. Beat until smooth, cover and set aside at room temperature until needed.

Spread the base of the tart shell with cherry jam and scatter over a handful of the pitted cherries. Spoon or pipe the frangipane mixture on top and spread level. Gently press the remaining cherries on top and scatter with the flaked almonds.

Bake on the middle shelf of the oven for about 40 minutes until the frangipane is risen, set and golden brown.

Leave to cool to room temperature and dust with icing sugar to serve.

★

Probationer's Pudding

BREAD & BUTTER PUDDING

This was a recipe submitted to *The Windsor Castle Cookery Book*, in aid of St George's School, by the then Prince of Wales. The book, put together for the 'Children of the Garter', has recipes from the Queen Mother, Princess Alexandra and the Duchess of Kent, and offers no explanation as to why this pudding is for the probationer.

— Serves 4 —

300ml full-fat milk

300ml double cream

1 vanilla pod, split lengthways

6 thick slices of white bread, crusts removed

75g unsalted butter, softened, plus extra for greasing

2–3 tablespoons marmalade (optional)

125g sultanas (or chopped prunes)

75g light muscovado sugar

6 eggs

icing sugar, for dusting

You will need

20 × 30cm ovenproof dish, greased with butter

continued overleaf

Pour the milk and cream into a pan, add the split vanilla pod and bring to the boil over a medium heat. Remove from the heat and leave to infuse for 30 minutes.

Meanwhile, generously spread the bread slices with butter and marmalade, if using. Cut each slice into triangular quarters and layer into the buttered ovenproof dish with the sultanas.

In a bowl, whisk together the sugar and eggs, then add the milk and cream and whisk to combine. Strain into a jug and pour into the dish around and over the bread. Leave to soak for 10 minutes.

Meanwhile, preheat the oven to 170°C/325°F/gas mark 3.

Bake the pudding in a roasting tin half-filled with boiling water for 30–40 minutes until the custard has set and the top is golden brown.

Dust with icing sugar and serve either hot or cold.

★

Gâteau en Surprise

This, according to Tschumi, was one of the Princess Royal's (Princess Mary, later the Countess of Harewood) favourite cakes. One look at the finished product, and you could see why. Cake. Hollowed out. Stuffed with ice cream. Covered with chocolate ganache. Hell, it's even got me excited.

— Serves 8 —

For the cake
50g unsalted butter, plus extra for greasing

150g plain flour, plus extra for dusting

6 eggs

150g caster sugar

1 teaspoon vanilla extract

50g ground almonds

1 teaspoon baking powder

a pinch of salt

For the filling
3 large scoops of vanilla ice cream

3 large scoops of chocolate ice cream

For the ganache
200g dark chocolate (60–70% cocoa solids), finely chopped

200ml double cream

To finish
75g flaked almonds, toasted

You will need
3 × 20cm cake tins

continued overleaf

Preheat the oven to 180°C/350°F/gas mark 4. Butter the cake tins and line the bases with discs of buttered baking paper. Lightly dust the insides of the tins with a little plain flour and tap out the excess.

Melt the butter and set aside.

Place the eggs in the bowl of a stand mixer, add the sugar and vanilla extract, and whisk on high speed for 3–4 minutes until the mixture has trebled in volume, is thick, pale, very light and will leave a ribbon trail when the whisk is lifted from the bowl. Sift the flour, ground almonds, baking powder and a pinch of salt into the bowl and, using a large metal spoon, gently fold into the egg mixture. Pour the melted butter around the inside edge of the bowl and gently fold in.

Divide the batter evenly between the prepared tins, spread level and bake on the middle shelf of the oven for about 20 minutes, or until golden, risen and a skewer inserted into the middle of the cakes comes out clean.

Cool the cakes in the tins for a couple of minutes and then turn out onto a wire cooling rack and leave until cold.

If the tops of the cakes are domed, slice off the dome using a serrated knife. Place one cake layer back in the bottom of a clean cake tin. Using a plate or bowl with a diameter of 15cm as a guide, cut a circle out of the middle of the second cake layer. Save the middle disc for something else and place the cake ring into the tin on top of the first cake layer. Freeze for 30 minutes.

Slightly soften the vanilla ice cream and spread into the gap in the middle of the cake ring. Return the cake to the freezer for 1 hour until the vanilla ice cream is firm.

Soften the chocolate ice cream and spread on top of the vanilla. Top with the third cake layer, gently pressing the cake layers together. Freeze again for at least 2 hours until solid.

To make the ganache, tip the chopped chocolate into a mixing bowl. Heat the cream until just boiling, pour over the chocolate and leave for 2 minutes. Stir until smooth, then leave to cool for 15 minutes. Whisk the ganache until smooth and thickened to a spreading consistency.

Roughly chop the toasted flaked almonds and tip into a tray.

Remove the gâteau from the tin and spread the sides with ganache. Roll the sides of the cake in the almonds to coat. Place the gâteau on a serving plate and spread the top with the remaining ganache. Either serve immediately or return to the freezer until ready to do so.

Rhubarb Fool

WITH GINGER BISCUITS & KING'S GINGER

There's nothing silly about this particular fool. It has long graced the regal table, alongside various syllabub and posset cousins, both sweetly satisfying and joyously simple. A great British dish, too, bringing together the joys of the pasture (we may moan about the rain, but it does make for the lushest of grass, which, in turn, means the richest of cream) with the fruits of the walled garden. The key is the balance between thrillingly tart rhubarb, sweetened juice and whipped cream. Oh, and a good glug of King's Ginger. Created to 'stimulate and revivify' King Edward VII while driving his 'horseless carriage', better known as a Daimler.

— Serves 6 —

600g forced rhubarb, washed and trimmed

150g caster sugar

grated zest and juice of 1 orange

600ml double cream

175g ginger biscuits

about 125ml King's Ginger liqueur

Preheat the oven to 180°C/350°F/gas mark 4.

Cut the rhubarb into 3–4cm lengths and place in an ovenproof dish. Sprinkle with the sugar, orange zest and juice, and mix to combine. Cover with a sheet of baking paper or foil and bake for about 30–40 minutes, depending on the thickness of the rhubarb stems, until soft. Leave to cool.

Strain the juice from the rhubarb and reserve. Pick out six pieces of rhubarb for decoration and set aside, then purée the remaining rhubarb in a food processor until nearly smooth.

Whip the cream until it forms soft peaks, not too firm, then fold in the cold rhubarb purée along with a few dribbles of the reserved juice. Don't mix too manically, there should be some ripples of rhubarb still visible.

Tip the ginger biscuits into a freezer bag and bash with a rolling pin until crushed into small pieces but not so fine as sand. Put a layer of the crushed biscuits into six wine glasses, then add a a splash of the ginger booze. Spoon the fool on top of the biscuits and finish with the reserved rhubarb pieces and a drizzle of the cooking juices.

Buckingham Palace Plum Pudding

The original recipe for Buckingham Palace Plum Pudding, found in Tschumi's *Royal Chef*, includes 30lb of Lisbon sugar, 40lb of raisins, 50lb of beef suet, 150 eggs, a bottle of rum and a bottle of brandy. 'Made for the Royal Household at Christmas', the recipe is 'sufficient for 150 small puddings, each weighing 2lb.' This might be a little excessive for most, so this recipe, direct from the royal kitchen, was shared by the late Queen in 2021 over Instagram. The mix should be made on 'Stir-up Sunday', the last Sunday before Advent begins, and left to mature. Times may have changed, but the quality remains the same. If you don't want to use alcohol, you can substitute the liquids for orange juice or cold tea.

— Makes two 1kg puddings —

250g raisins

250g currants

185g sultanas

150g mixed peel

250g suet or vegetarian suet

250g breadcrumbs

90g flour

12g mixed spice

180g demerara sugar

2 whole eggs

275ml beer

40ml dark rum

40ml brandy

50ml butter, melted, for greasing

brandy sauce or cream, to serve

You will need

2 × 1kg pudding bowls

First, combine all the dry ingredients and stir them up. Add the eggs and liquids. Stir it all up.

Grease the pudding bowls with melted butter. Press the cake mix into the bowls and cover with a circle of baking paper. Cover the puddings with muslin or foil and place each in a deep saucepan filled with boiling water up to three-quarters of the basins' height. Cover the saucepan with foil and steam for 6 hours, refilling the water when needed.

Once cooled, wrap the puddings and store in a cool, dry place until Christmas.

On Christmas Day, reheat your pudding in a bain-marie for 3–4 hours. Remove from the basin using a round-bladed knife or palette knife, flip out onto a plate and flambé. Serve with brandy sauce and cream.

Crème Brûlée

This recipe is another from *The Royal Blue & Gold Cook Book*, a charity tome written by the Marchioness of Cambridge, whose husband, George, was a nephew of Queen Mary. The recipe comes from George VI and Queen Elizabeth, and is included along with one for Southern Fried Chicken from Clark Gable. This custard is cooked very slowly in the oven like a crème caramel.

— Serves 4 —

300ml double cream

3 egg yolks

1 tablespoon caster sugar

seeds of 1 vanilla pod

2 teaspoons icing sugar

Preheat the oven to 160°C/325°F/gas mark 3.

Put the cream in a medium bowl and add the egg yolks, one at a time. Mix in the caster sugar and the seeds of the vanilla pod. Mix thoroughly, but do not let the mixture become frothy. Pour into individual custard cups or dariole moulds.

Bake in the oven for 45 minutes until the custard is firmly set.

Sprinkle the tops with the icing sugar and either glaze under a hot grill or use a kitchen blow torch, being careful that the tops do not get too brown.

Chill for several hours.

Gugelhupf

This is one of those cakes claimed by a few different countries – in this case, Austria, Germany and Switzerland. All have their own take on this classic spiced, fruited, yeasted cake. It featured on the menus of Queen Victoria, who was introduced to it by Prince Albert. At a dinner given by the Queen at Windsor on 14 May 1874, for His Imperial Majesty, Tsar Alexander II of Russia, it appeared as *Les Couglauffes aux Raisins, Sauce Abricot*. The dinner had an added frisson in that the young Victoria had taken rather a fancy to the then Grand Duke at a Windsor ball in 1839. 'I really am quite in love with the Grand Duke; he is a dear, delightful young man,' she sighed in her journal. 'The Grand Duke is so very strong, that in running round, you must follow quickly and after that you are whisked round like in a Valse, which is very pleasant... I never enjoyed myself more. We were all so merry; I got to bed by a quarter to three but could not sleep till five.' The feeling was apparently, mutual. But it was not to be. His father, Nicholas I, heard of the nascent romance, and summoned his son back home to Russia. He left his dog, Kazbek, as a goodbye present. Lard is traditionally used here, and gives a wonderful texture, but I've substituted butter instead.

— Serves 10 —

150g sultanas

2 tablespoons dark rum

10g dried active yeast

200ml full-fat milk

125g caster sugar

350g plain flour

¼ teaspoon ground cinnamon

1 teaspoon vanilla extract

zest of 1 lemon

a big pinch of sea salt

2 eggs, plus 1 egg yolk

175g unsalted butter, softened, plus extra, melted, for the tin

100g whole almonds

icing sugar, for dusting

You will need

a large bundt tin

Soak the sultanas in the rum for at least 4 hours, preferably overnight.

Put the yeast into the bowl of a stand mixer. Heat the milk until warm, then add to the bowl along with 1 teaspoon of the sugar. Mix well, then leave for about 15 minutes until a bubbling crust has formed.

Add the rest of sugar to the bowl along with the flour, cinnamon, vanilla, lemon zest and a pinch of sea salt. Beat the eggs and yolk together and add to the bowl, along with the butter. Mix, starting slowly, with a dough hook attachment if you have one, until all is combined, then continue mixing for 3–4 minutes, until smooth. Cover the bowl with a damp towel and leave in a warm place to rise for an hour. It should double in size.

While the dough is rising, put the bundt tin in the fridge to chill, then brush with melted butter. Scatter the whole almonds at the bottom of the tin.

Add the rum-soaked fruit to the dough and mix again until all combined. Put the dough into the prepared tin, pushing it down and making sure it's even on top. Cover with a damp towel and leave for a further hour.

Meanwhile, preheat the oven to 170°C/325°F/gas mark 3.

Bake the *gugelhupf* for about 45 minutes until a skewer inserted into the middle comes out clean. Allow to cool, then turn out onto a wire rack. Ensure the cake is completely cold before dusting with icing sugar.

Rødgrød

This Danish berry pudding, with its deep red hue, was a great favourite of Queen Alexandra (formerly Princess Alexandra of Denmark). Although her husband was less than keen – 'King Edward preferred savouries and considered *rødgrød* far too sweet to finish off with at supper,' recalled Tschumi. It was served with cream and tiny, sweet biscuits made by the confectionery chef. Traditionally, it was thickened with Danish sago flour, but even in 1903 this was near impossible to find outside Denmark. I use cornflour instead.

— Serves 6 —

1kg red berries (raspberries, strawberries, redcurrants, blackcurrants)

500ml water

140g caster sugar

250ml claret

30g cornflour dissolved in 120ml water

double cream and shortbread biscuits, to serve

Put the berries in a non-reactive saucepan along with the water, bring to the boil, then simmer gently until the fruit is on the edge of falling apart. Strain through a fine sieve, making sure you really extract every last drop, and return the juice to the pan.

Add the sugar to the juice in the pan and stir gently over a medium heat until dissolved.

Add the claret and simmer for a few minutes, then stir in the cornflour mixture and simmer for a further minute or two to cook out the cornflour. Pour into six dessert glasses and refrigerate for 1 hour.

Serve with lashings of double cream and some shortbread biscuits.

Bombe Glacée

This was served at the wedding breakfast of Princess Elizabeth and Lieutenant Phillip Mountbatten, on Thursday 2 November 1947. As rationing was still very much in force, the menu was relatively restrained. Sole, partridge, then pudding. You can make your own ice cream, but it's rather easier to use good shop-bought stuff. Just avoid the 'soft-scoop'.

— Serves 6 —

100g chocolate-coated honeycomb

250g digestive biscuits

75g unsalted butter

2–3 teaspoons neutral oil

2 × 500ml tubs of good-quality vanilla ice cream

1 × 500ml tub of good-quality chocolate ice cream

300ml raspberry ice cream

You will need

2 litre Pyrex mixing bowl

Crumble the chocolate-coated honeycomb and digestives into a food processor and pulse until they become sandy crumbs, then tip into a mixing bowl. Melt the butter, add to the crumbs and mix until combined.

Brush the inside of the Pyrex bowl with oil (not butter) and line with a double thickness of clingfilm, leaving some excess film hanging over the sides. Press the crumb mixture over the inside of the bowl to make a firm shell with an even thickness. Freeze for at least 30 minutes until solid.

Slightly soften 600ml of vanilla ice cream, then use a spoon to press the ice cream into a smooth and even layer over the frozen crumbs. Return the bowl to the freezer for at least 30 minutes until the ice cream is completely frozen again. Repeat with all of the chocolate ice cream to make a second layer of ice cream. Freeze for 30 minutes again. Use the remaining vanilla ice cream to make a third layer and freeze for 30 minutes. Finally, fill the middle of the bombe with raspberry ice cream, cover and freeze for at least 1 hour, or until ready to serve.

Using a knife, trim the crumbs and smooth the top of the ice cream bombe so that it will sit level on a serving plate when it is turned out. To remove the bombe from the bowl, gently ease a palette knife in between the bowl and the clingfilm, place a serving plate on top and – holding onto both the plate and bowl – turn the bowl upside down onto the plate. Gently pull on the clingfilm to release the bombe from the bowl. If the bombe is very stubborn to drop out of the bowl, dip the bowl in a sink of hot water for 10 seconds. Serve the bombe cut into wedges – perhaps with hot chocolate sauce to pour over.

Mango Melba

This is my mother, Queen Camilla's, take on *Pêches Melba*.

— Serves 4 —

2 ripe mangoes, peeled and thinly sliced

500ml good-quality vanilla ice cream

For the sauce

2 tablespoons water

1 teaspoon cornflour

50g raspberries

1 tablespoon caster sugar

To serve

125ml double cream, whipped to soft peaks

blanched almonds, chopped

To make the melba sauce, blend the cornflour with the measured water in a small pan until smooth. Add the raspberries and sugar, and cook very gently until the mixture thickens. The resulting sauce can be strained through a sieve, if desired.

Arrange the mango in individual glasses, then cover with the sauce and top with 2 scoops of ice cream each. Decorate with piped rosettes of whipped cream and chopped almonds, and serve.

Royal Kitchens

'I remember on my first days at Windsor thinking how much the kitchen reminded me of a chapel with its high domed ceiling, its feeling of airiness and light, and the gleam of copper at each end of the room.' Gabriel Tschumi was writing in 1899, but things have changed little to this day. In fact, it's near impossible not to be moved by the sheer scale of the room. Along with its 750 years of history. Here, in this majestic space, royal chefs from Charles Elmé Francatelli and Messieurs Misson and Menager to Ronald Aubrey and Mark Flanagan have cooked up feasts, banquets, TV suppers and midnight snacks. 'History is everywhere here,' says Flanagan. 'It's so inspiring to work in such a beautiful place.'

Of course, the great fireplaces at each end, both large enough to roast a whole ox, are no longer seething with burning coals. Although those spits remain. And the white walls are still hung with dozens of burnished copper stock pots, pans and jelly moulds, some bearing VR, the insignia of Queen Victoria. A simple clock, above the words G.IV. REX.1838, commemorates the renovations started by George IV. Metal gas ranges have replaced coal fires and there's an extraction system so powerful it whips the words right out of your mouth. All the culinary mod cons are here, and it's still one of the world's great kitchens. A working one, too.

The Buckingham Palace kitchen is rather more modern, but still has more of those copper pots and pans. The old fireplace remains, and the rotisserie, operated by a ingenious system of pulleys and weights. 'The iPhone of its day,' laughs Flanagan. All is calm here, just as it was in Tschumi's day, where the kitchens had 'the discipline of the barracks room'. They're a long way removed from the original Buckingham Palace kitchens, built by George IV, where raw sewage seeped through the floor, and the putrid, searingly hot air was thick with smoke and choking fumes. Prince Albert not only moved the kitchen in 1851, but made it bigger, cleaner and better ventilated too.

Of course, these kitchens don't feed just the royal family, but over 800 people daily, from private secretaries and ladies in waiting to valets, pages, dressers, maids, electricians, plumbers, IT staff, policemen and gardeners who make up the royal household. Under Victoria there was a permanent kitchen staff of forty-five. These days there are twenty-one. Still, the sense of awe remains. 'You are sometimes cooking in the same pots as Carême,' says Flanagan with a smile. Historical kitchens, then, where the past is ever-present.

Chocolate Bavarois

This recipe comes from Gabriel Tschumi, and was served at Queen Victoria's Garden Party, held on 11 July 1900. I've updated the recipe a little here, as the original seemed cloyingly sweet.

— Makes 6 —

3 gelatine leaves

500ml full-fat milk

120g good-quality dark chocolate, grated

4 egg yolks

200g caster sugar

280ml double cream, plus extra to serve

a handful of raspberries or strawberries, in summer (or blackberries in autumn), to serve

You will need

6 × 120ml aluminium pudding moulds

Soak the gelatine leaves in cold water. Put the moulds in the freezer.

Heat the milk in a saucepan until it just starts to simmer, then add the chocolate and stir until thoroughly melted and combined.

In a separate bowl, whisk the yolks and the sugar together, then add to the chocolate milk, stirring constantly over a low heat for about 5 minutes until it starts to get thick.

Squeeze out the gelatine leaves, add to the chocolate custard and remove from the heat. Leave to cool for 20 minutes.

Whisk 280ml of the double cream to soft peaks, then slowly, tablespoon by tablespoon, fold into the chocolate custard.

Remove the moulds from the freezer, divide mixture among them and return to the freezer for 30 minutes.

Pour a little extra double cream onto 6 individual dishes, then unmould the bavarois on top and serve with seasonal fruit on the side.

Pudding au Pain et aux Cerises

Another recipe from Mildred Dorothy Nicholls (see page 124), somewhat adapted for the modern kitchen. The joy is you can use frozen cherries, and thus eat it all year round.

— Serves 6 —

For the puddings

25g unsalted butter, softened, plus extra for greasing

2 teaspoons plain flour

175g fresh fine white breadcrumbs

150ml full-fat milk

200g frozen pitted cherries, defrosted

60g caster sugar

4 eggs, separated

1 teaspoon vanilla or lemon extract

a pinch of salt

For the cherry sauce

250g frozen pitted cherries, defrosted

50g caster sugar

juice of ½ lemon

100ml water

You will need

6 × 150ml ovenproof pudding moulds

Preheat the oven to 150°C/300°F/gas mark 2.

To make the puddings, grease the moulds with butter and place a disc of buttered baking paper in the bottom of each. Lightly dust the insides of the moulds with plain flour and tap out any excess.

Tip the breadcrumbs into a mixing bowl, add the milk, mix to combine and leave to soak for 15 minutes.

Cut the cherries in half and pat dry on kitchen paper.

Beat the butter and sugar until smooth. Add the egg yolks, one at a time, mixing well after each addition. Add the vanilla or lemon extract and soaked breadcrumbs, and mix again to combine.

In another bowl, whisk the egg whites with a pinch of salt until they will hold stiff but not dry peaks.

Using a large metal spoon, lightly fold the halved cherries into the breadcrumb mixture. Fold in a spoonful of the egg whites to lighten the mixture, then carefully fold in the remainder.

Divide the mixture evenly between the prepared moulds, filling each one to within 1cm

continued overleaf

from the top. Spread level with the back of a spoon. Tightly cover each pudding mould with a square of buttered foil and place in a roasting tin. Pour boiling water into the tin to come halfway up the sides of the basins and bake the puddings for about 35 minutes until risen, golden and cooked through. A wooden skewer will come out clean when pushed into the middle of the puddings.

Meanwhile, prepare the cherry sauce. Tip the cherries into a saucepan, add the sugar, lemon juice and measured water, and cook over a low heat, stirring often, for about 10 minutes until the cherries are very soft but still hold their shape and the sauce is syrupy.

Leave the puddings to rest for 5 minutes, then use a round-bladed or palette knife to carefully turn the puddings out onto serving plates. Serve with the hot cherry sauce.

✳

Crêpes au Naturel

A favourite of George V. It's a classic pancake recipe, with a little added cream and brandy.

— Makes 10 —

100g plain white flour
a pinch of salt
2 large eggs
3 tablespoons double cream
300ml milk
a hearty jig of brandy

30g butter, melted
neutral oil, for greasing

To serve
caster sugar, to taste
2 lemons, quartered

In a large bowl or jug, beat together the flour, salt, eggs and cream until thoroughly blended. Add the milk, brandy and melted butter and stir well. Strain through a sieve, then allow to stand in the fridge for 2–3 hours.

Wipe a medium frying pan or crêpe pan with oiled kitchen paper and heat well over a medium heat. Pour in a small ladleful of batter and swirl it around pan so it covers the base. Cook the crêpe for about 1 minute on each side before turning out onto a plate. Roll and serve immediately with lemon and sugar, to taste.

Repeat to cook the remaining crêpes.

Bibliography

Anonymous, *The Private Life of the Queen* (D. Appleton and Company, 1896)

Aubrey, Ronald, *A Royal Chef's Notebook* (Gresham Books, 1978)

Bradford, Sarah, *George VI* (Weidenfeld & Nicholson, 1989)

Cambridge, The Marchioness of, *The Royal Blue & Gold Cook Book* (Jupiter Books, 1974)

Cowles, Virginia, *Gay Monarch: The Life and Pleasures of Edward VII* (Harper & Brothers, 1956)

Currah, Ann, *Chef To Queen Victoria: The Recipes of Charles Elmé Francatelli* (William Kimber, 1973)

Escoffier, Auguste, *The Escoffier Cookbook and Guide to the Fine Art of Cookery* (Clarkson Potter, 1969)

Flanagan, Mark and Griffiths, Edward *A Royal Cookbook: Seasonal recipes from Buckingham Palace* (Royal Collection Trust, 2014)

Flanagan, Mark and Cuthbertson, Kathryn, *Royal Teas: Seasonal recipes from Buckingham Palace* (Royal Collection Trust, 2017)

Gore, John, *King George V: A Personal Memoir* (John Murray, 1941)

Gouffe, Jules, *The Royal Cookery Book* (Sampson Low, Son, and Marston, 1869)

Gray, Annie, *The Greedy Queen: Eating with Victoria* (Profile Books, 2017)

Groom, Susanne, *At The King's Table: Royal Dining Through the Ages* (Merrell, 2013)

Haller, Henry, *The White House Family Cookbook* (Random House, 1987)

Hardman, Robert, *Queen Of Our Times: The Life of Elizabeth II, 1926–2022* (Macmillan, 2022)

Hibbert, Christopher, *Edward VII: The Last Victorian King* (Griffin, 2007)

Hoey, Brian, *The Royal Yacht Britannia: Inside the Queen's Floating Palace* (Patrick Stephens Limited, 1995)

Jones, Kathryn, *For The Royal Table: Dining at the Palace* (Royal Collection Trust 2008)

Keppel, Sonia, *Edwardian Daughter* (Hamish Hamilton, 1958)

Magnus, Philip, *King Edward The Seventh* (John Murray, 1964)

McKee, Alma, *To Set Before A Queen* (Arlington Books, 1963)

McKee, Alma, *Mrs McKee's Royal Cookery Book* (Arlington Books, 1964)

Murray, Christina, *A Taste of Mey: Recipes and Memories* (Queen Elizabeth Castle of Mey Trust, 2011)

Nicholson, Harold, *King George V* (Constable and Co, 1952)

Oliver, Charles, *Dinner at Buckingham Palace: Secrets & Recipes from the reign of Queen Victoria to Queen Elizabeth II*, edited and compiled by Paul Fishman and Fiorella Busoni (Metro Books, 2003)

Ponsonby, Sir Frederick, *Recollections of Three Reigns* (Eyre & Spottiswoode, 1951)

Pope-Hennessy, James, *The Quest for Queen Mary*, edited by Hugo Vickers (Hodder & Stoughton, 2018)

Prud'Homme, Alex, *Dinner With The President: Food, Politics, and a History of Breaking Bread at the White House* (Alfred A. Knopf, 2023)

Ridley, Jane, *Bertie: A Life of Edward VII* (Chatto & Windus, 2012)

Ridley, Jane, *George V: Never a Dull Moment* (Chatto & Windus, 2021)

Rose, Kenneth, *King George V* (Weidenfeld & Nicholson, 1983)

Strong, Sir Roy, *Feast: A History of Grand Eating* (Jonathan Cape, 2002)

Tooley, Sarah A. Southall, *The Personal Life of Queen Victoria* (Arcadia Press, 1897)

Tschumi, Gabriel, *Royal Chef: Forty Years with Royal Households* (William Kimber, 1954)

Victoria, HM The Queen, *Leaves From The Journal of Our Life In The Highlands* (Smith, Elder and Company, 1868)

Windsor Castle Parents of Choristers of St George's Chapel, *The Windsor Castle Cookery Book: Entertaining With the Children of the Garter* (Nicole Crossley-Holland, 1996)

Windsor, The Duke of, *A King's Story: The Memoirs of HRH The Duke of Windsor KG* (Cassell & Co, 1951)

Ziegler, Philip, *King Edward VIII: The Official Biography* (Collins, 1990)

Suppliers

Meat

H G Walter
www.hgwalter.com
One of the country's best butchers, and one of my favourites too.

The Ethical Butcher
www.ethicalbutcher.co.uk
Excellent quality British meat, bred on farms that embrace regenerative agriculture.

Turner and George
www.turnerandgeorge.co.uk
These men really know their meat, supplied by small, independent farmers, with their beef dry-aged on site.

Hannan Meats
www.hannanmeats.com
Peter Hannan's salt-aged Glenarm beef is some of the best I've ever tasted.

Fish

Wright Brothers
www.thewrightbrothers.co.uk
A huge selection of top-quality oysters, shellfish and fish. Sustainably sourced, and delivered across the UK.

Rockfish
www.therockfish.co.uk
Not only does Mitch Tonks sell the very freshest fish, sustainably fished from Brixham every weekday morning, he also does some incredible English tinned fish.

Chalkstream
www.chalkstreamfoods.co.uk
Farmed rainbow trout that tastes pure and clean, thanks to slow growth in gin-clear Hampshire chalk stream water.

Flour

Shipton Mill
www.shipton-mill.com
You'll find every kind of organic stone-ground flour here, as well as yeasts and olive oils.

Farmshops

Farmshop
Based in Bruton, this specialises in beef, pork and lamb from their Somerset farm, as well as some cracking West country cheese and charcuterie.

Highgrove
www.highgrovegardens.com
Organic food from the King's Gloucestershire estate, you'll find everything from jams and biscuits to sweets, mustards and chutneys.

Windsor Castle Farm Shop
www.windsorfarmshop.co.uk
Slow reared, traditional breed beef, pork and lamb from the Royal Estates, and some good cheese and dairy too.

Sandringham
www.sandringhamestate.co.uk
Beer, honey, chocolate, tea and toffee, along with a good range of sweets and biscuits.

Daylesford
www.daylesford.com
Carole Bamford was a sustainable farm shop pioneer, and Daylesford gets better by the year. All the organic meat comes from the Bamford's estates, while fruit and vegetables come from their market garden. Their cheeses are sublime (don't miss the Double Gloucester), along with pretty much everything else.

Smoked Fish

Brown and Forrest
www.brownandforrest.co.uk
A really great Somerset smokery, who source the best fish, cheese and meat from trusted local suppliers and work wonders over their brick kiln.

Severn and Wye
www.severnandwye.co.uk
If you are going to eat smoked salmon, then theirs is one of the very best. I love their whole smoked eels too.

Secret Smokehouse
www.secretsmokehouse.co.uk
PGA certificated 'London' cure salmon smokers (they also do a fine smoked trout and mackerel). They supply the likes of The Ritz, Wilton's, The Fat Duck, Core and Claude Bosi. They are also pioneers of 'land-based' farmed salmon (i.e. which doesn't pollute the coastal waters), which for me, could be the future.

Caviar

King's Fine Foods
www.kingsfinefood.co.uk
Few people know as much about caviar as Laura King, the 'queen of caviar'. The only place to buy the best farmed caviar in the world.

Salt

Maldon
www.maldonsalt.com
Wonderful texture and good, clean flavour

Halen Môn
www.halenmon.com
Another salt classic, crunchy yet soft enough to crush between the fingers.

Ironware

Netherton Foundry
www.netherton-foundry.co.uk
Traditional cast and spun iron cookware, handmade in Shropshire. I have two frying pans from them, and use them every day. They last a lifetime and never let you down.

Cheesemongers

The Courtyard Diary
www.thecourtyarddairy.co.uk
A brilliant Yorkshire cheesemonger that has been utterly vital in supporting artisan cheese producers. Legends, in every way.

La Fromagerie
www.lafromagerie.co.uk
One of the originals, and still one of the best, Patricia Michelson's three shops are London classics. They have a huge range of continental cheese, perfectly kept, but an equally impressive collection of British beauties too.

The Fine Cheese Co
www.finecheese.co.uk
A Bath institution. Great selection of British (and European) cheeses. And they keep them beautifully too.

Neal's Yard Dairy
www.nealsyarddairy.co.uk
Another London legend, and pioneers of supporting great British cheeses too.

Index

About the Author

Tom Parker Bowles has been an award-winning food writer for more than 20 years, is the author of eight books on food (including the bestselling Fortnum & Mason cookbooks) and is the restaurant critic for *The Mail on Sunday*. He is also a contributing editor for *Esquire*, *Country Life* and *Condé Nast Traveller*, plus a regular judge on the BBC's *Masterchef*. Tom is a godson of King Charles III, and his mother, Camilla, is Queen.

𝕏 @tomparkerbowles

✳

About the Photographer

Born in London, award-winning food and drink photographer John Carey has worked on books with Gordon Ramsay, the Ritz and Claridge's amongst many others. John's eye for detail and passion for photography, food and drink mean he has a broad client base that includes some of the most prestigious chefs, restaurants, hotels, book publishers and brands in the world.

◉ @johncareyphoto

✳

About the Illustrator

Alice Pattullo is an illustrator originally from Newcastle Upon Tyne, who lives and works in East London. Alice works on commissioned illustrations for a wide variety of clients as well as producing limited edition screen prints which she exhibits and sells in the UK.

◉ @alicepattullo

Acknowledgements

This book, as ever, is a group effort, and would not have been possible without such an incredible bunch of talented people. I just scrawl the words. The real magic comes from elsewhere.

I'd like to thank TM the King and Queen Camilla for all of their help, guidance and inspiration.

Stephanie Jackson at Octopus, my brilliant publisher, at long last we have been able to work together. It's been a joy. Pauline Bache, who has watched over, organised, edited and arranged every part of this book. And Creative Director Jonathan Christie, who shaped its look and feel. Thanks to Chloë Johnson-Hill and her marketing and PR team; Marianne Laidlaw, Veronique de Sutter and their colleagues in sales for the UK and worldwide; Peter Hunt in production and all at Octopus who have contributed along the way.

To John Carey, photographer, Cure fanatic and an industry great. Who knew a photoshoot could actually be fun? Huge thanks also to Annie Rigg, chef and author (but definitely not a 'home economist'), who cooked, tested most of the recipes in the book and offered essential advice and guidance throughout along with Hattie Baker. And to Tamsin Weston for the brilliant props.

And of course, Alice Pattullo, the illustrator, for all her beautiful drawings.

A massive thank you to Mark Flanagan, Royal Chef, who went out of his way to help, despite being in the middle of about ten different menus every day; his insight was crucial, his knowledge immense. And Stuart Major, Head Chef at Clarence House, for all of his recipes too.

Thanks also to Bill Stockting and Julie Crocker and everyone at the Royal Archive in Windsor.

Cleyenne Lazarotto-Miotto, for her endless support, and for reading countless early drafts. And being refreshingly direct.

Hugo Vickers, for advice and quite a few recipes.

Tobyn Andreae, for all of his help.

Matthew Fort, Jeremy Lee, Jamie Sutherland, Tom Pemberton, John Williams, Gavin Rankin and Mark Hix for their recipes.

ASTER

First published in Great Britain in 2024 by
Aster, an imprint of
Octopus Publishing Group Ltd
Carmelite House,
50 Victoria Embankment
London EC4Y 0DZ
www.octopusbooks.co.uk

An Hachette UK Company
www.hachette.co.uk

The right of Tom Parker Bowles to be
identified as the author of this Work has been
asserted by him in accordance with the
Copyright, Designs & Patents Act 1988.

ISBN 978-1-78325-606-8

A CIP catalogue record for this book is
available from the British Library.

Printed and bound in China.

10 9 8 7 6 5 4 3 2 1

Publisher: Stephanie Jackson
Creative director: Jonathan Christie
Photographer: John Carey
Illustrator: Alice Pattullo
Senior editor: Pauline Bache
Copy editor: Emily Preece-Morrison
Food stylist: Annie Rigg
Food styling assistant: Hattie Baker
Props stylist: Tamsin Weston
Senior production manager: Peter Hunt

Every effort has been made to identify
relevant copyright holders for historical
recipes in this book. Please contact the
publisher should any omission have been
made and we will be happy to rectify it at the
next printing.

Cookery notes

Standard level spoon measurements
    are used in all recipes.
1 tablespoon = one 15 ml spoon
1 teaspoon = one 5 ml spoon

Eggs should be free-range and medium unless
otherwise stated. Milk should be full fat
unless otherwise stated. Fresh herbs should be
used unless otherwise stated. Ovens should be
preheated to the specific temperature – if
using a fan-assisted oven, follow
manufacturer's instructions for adjusting the
time and the temperature.